A Practical Course on Operating Systems

Colin J. Theaker

Senior Lecturer in Computer Science,
University of Manchester

Graham R. Brookes

Senior Lecturer in Computer Science,
University of Sheffield

First published 1983 by
THE MACMILLAN PRESS LTD
London and Basingstoke
Companies and representatives
throughout the world

Printed in Great Britain by
Unwin Brothers Limited
The Gresham Press, Old Woking, Surrey

ISBN 0 333 34678 5
     0 333 34679 3 pbk

Contents

PART 2 OPERATING SYSTEM TECHNIQUES

Preface

An operating system is one of the most important pieces of software to go into any modern computer system, irrespective of its size, yet because systems seek to be transparent to the computer user, much mystique surrounds their design. As computer systems increase in complexity, particularly at the microprocessor level, more complexity appears in the system software. The primary objective of this book is to dispel the mystique associated with operating system design, and to provide a greater practical understanding of the design and implementation of operating systems.

The contents of this book are derived from a number of courses of lectures given to undergraduate students of computer science. In its entirety it provides suitable material for a full course on operating systems for students who have a basic grounding in computer science, or who have some practical experience of computing. However, less detailed courses may be derived by choosing a sub-section of the chapters. For example, the first four chapters provide a simple overview of the structure of an operating system, and can therefore be used as material for a lower level course, which seeks to provide a general discussion of the nature and role of an operating system.

The first four chapters also provide the background for the more detailed considerations that follow. This begins with an examination of scheduling principles and the algorithms associated with scheduling. The treatment of memory management traces much of the evolutionary path of operating systems, from the need for base-limit registers to the design of paged segmented machines. Subsequent chapters examine the problems of resource management, including the protection of resources and the avoidance of deadlocks. The problems of concurrency are then examined, and a number of techniques for achieving cooperation and synchronisation of processes are described. Finally, the interface most familiar to the user, namely the job control language is considered.

Throughout the book there are exercises for the student at the end of each chapter, together with references in which the student can find more detailed information on specific topics.

The authors wish to acknowledge the assistance and encouragement of colleagues, in particular to Dr G. R. Frank, whose lectures on operating systems at the University of Manchester provided much inspiration for this book, and more generally to Professor D. Morris and Professor F. H. Sumner. They thank Professor D. Howarth for helpful suggestions in earlier drafts. Finally, they thank Margaret Huzar for her patience in typing the manuscript of this book throughout its many stages.

Part 1 Design of an Operating System

1 Basic Operating System Concepts

We shall begin our consideration of operating systems by asking the following questions:

    (1)   What is an operating system?
    (2)   Why are operating systems needed?
    (3)   Do situations exist when they are not needed?
    (4)   How would an operating system be designed?

The first part of this book aims to provide answers to these questions. During the course of this, we shall present a simple overview of the design of an operating system. The subject is developed in more detail in the second part of the book, where particular problem areas are discussed together with algorithms used within operating systems. Whenever possible, the book contains illustrations of a theoretical operating system written in the style of the language Pascal.

Take the first question — 'what is an operating system?'. In simple terms it is just a program, but its size and complexity will depend on a number of factors, most notably the characteristics of the computer system, the facilities it has to provide and the nature of the applications it has to support. For example, the operating system for a single user microprocessor can be relatively simple in comparison with that for a large multi-user mainframe computer.

Regardless of size, the operating system is usually the first program loaded into the computer when the machine is started. Once loaded, some portions of it remain permanently in memory while the computer is running jobs. Other portions of the operating system are swapped in and out of memory when facilities are required by the users.

To answer the second — 'Why are operating systems needed' — it is worth stating the basic objectives that an operating system is seeking to attain:

(1) To provide a higher level interface so that the hardware of the computer becomes more readily usable.

(2) To provide the most cost effective use of the hardware of the computer.

Operating systems attempt to satisfy both of these objectives although, in practice, these requirements are not mutually exclusive and so a compromise in design has to be made. In consequence, there are many types of operating system. In this book we shall seek to illustrate the principles behind a range of operating systems rather than provide a full consideration of any specific system.

As with most complex pieces of software, it is possible to regard the structure of an operating system as a layered object, analogous to, say, an onion. At the centre is a nucleus of basic facilities, to which additional layers are added as required to provide more sophisticated facilities. Some modern operating systems, such as VME/B for the ICL 2900 (Keedy, 1976; Huxtable and Pinkerton, 1977) and UNIX (Ritchie and Thompson, 1974), exhibit this neatly layered structure and some machines even provide hardware support for such a layered organisation.

Rather than starting with such a system and decomposing it to identify the important components of an operating system, the approach we intend to take in this book is to concentrate initially on the nucleus of the system. Starting at the most primitive level, the hardware, we shall consider the design of a very simple operating system, examining its limitations and hence identifying what improvements and enhancements would be required to provide a powerful and sophisticated system. We thus intend to build up the design of an operating system in an evolutionary manner. In many respects, this reflects the historical development that has led to the present structure of modern operating systems.

This book is divided into two parts. In the first, we examine the needs of a very simple system and develop its design so that, by the end of part 1, the framework of an operating system has been established. In the second part, we identify the deficiencies of this system and examine techniques and algorithms that can be used to resolve these problems.

1.1 GENERAL FEATURES

Initially it is necessary to identify the sort of services that an operating system might provide to help the user run a program. These are somewhat analogous to the existence of assemblers and compilers that allow a user to write a program in languages other than binary code.

(1) Convenient input/output operations.

Users do not want to know the details of how a particular peripheral has to be driven in order to read or print a character. Clearly, a higher-level interface than this must be provided for the user.

(2) Fault monitoring.

No matter how proficient the programmer, it is impossible for anyone to write faultless programs all the time. It is therefore essential for the system to cater for errors arising in a program. When errors are detected, the operating system intervenes to print suitable monitoring information to help the user find the source of the fault. Various levels of monitoring information may be printed, some by the operating system, some by the compiler or run-time support system of the programming language.

(3) Multi-access.

Allowing several people to use the computer simultaneously is more convenient for the users, even though some users might suffer a longer response time at their terminal than they would if they had sole use of the computer.

(4) File systems.

The operating system maintains the directory and security of a user's files. Centralised control is necessary in order to allow several users to share the same hardware while maintaining a secure file system where the files of each user are protected from invalid access. An operating system might also provide utilities for accessing and manipulating the files (for example, editors).

1.2 PERFORMANCE CONSIDERATIONS

An important requirement of operating systems is to make the most cost-effective use of the computer hardware. This was particularly important in the early days of computing when the cost of even the most primitive of machines was quite substantial. Although technological advances have made modern microprocessor-based systems far more cost-effective, the problem of achieving good performance still remains with the larger mini and mainframe machines. In examining the problem of achieving good performance from a computer system, consider the system shown in figure 1.1.

To allow each user sole access to the computer hardware would mean in practice that the computer would be idle for long periods of time. For example, when the user was loading a program into the machine, it would be doing no other useful work. Even when a computer is running a job its efficiency may be very poor. Consider the example of running a simple assembler. The assembler might be organised to read a card from the card reader, generate the necessary instruction and plant it in memory, and print the line of assembly code on the

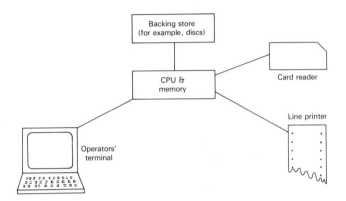

Figure 1.1 A simple computer system

lineprinter. Thus, in the sequence of processing each line there are three phases of operation:

| INPUT PHASE | PROCESS PHASE | OUTPUT PHASE |
(Read a card)   (Assemble the instructions)   (Print the line)

Assuming that the computer system has the characteristics of, say, a large minicomputer:

Card reader   300 cards/min
Lineprinter   300 lines/min
Central processing unit (CPU)   1 μs/instruction

Also, assuming that it takes about 10000 instructions to assemble each line, then the times for each of the three phases to process a card are:

(1) Input phase   200 ms
(2) Process phase   (10000 * 1) μs = 10 ms
(3) Output phase   200 ms

The CPU, which is only actively in use during the process phase, is busy for only 10 ms in every 410 ms.

The efficiency for CPU utilisation is defined by the following formula:

$$\text{Efficiency} = \frac{\text{Useful computing time}}{\text{Total time used}} * 100 \quad \text{per cent}$$

Using the characteristics above yields an efficiency given by:

$$\text{Efficiency} = \frac{10}{410} * 100 \simeq 2.4 \text{ per cent}$$

It is clearly very ineffective to use the CPU at such a low efficiency.

1.3 INPUT/OUTPUT LIMITED JOBS

We can readily see some possible improvements that might increase the utilisation of the computer system. It has been assumed in the calculations that the input phase (that is, the card reader) was started only when the process and output phases were complete. This would be achieved with the following control sequence for the card reader:

```
read card : REPEAT
                start reader
                WHILE reader not finished DO nothing
                UNTIL reader not in error

            process card
```

This sequence, which results in the timing shown in figure 1.2, has the disadvantage that the card reader is idle during the time when the card is being processed and printed.

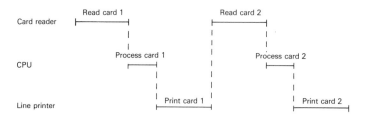

Figure 1.2 Process sequence for a simple system

The obvious way to speed this up is to copy the card image on to an intermediate area from where it can be processed and then to restart the reader immediately. The sequence that controls the card reader now becomes:

```
read card : REPEAT
                    IF card not available AND reader not running
                    THEN start reader
                    WHILE reader not finished DO nothing
                    UNTIL reader not in error

                    copy the card
                    start reader
```

This produces the sequence illustrated in figure 1.3.

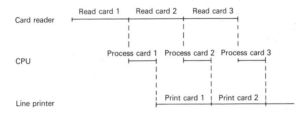

Figure 1.3 Process sequence for input/output-limited system

The peripherals are now kept busy all the time and a card would be processed on average every 200 ms. The CPU efficiency is still not significantly improved, however, being given by

$$\text{Efficiency} = \frac{10}{200} * 100 \simeq 5 \text{ per cent}$$

In this situation, the average time to process a card within the system is the time needed by the largest of the three phases of the operation; that is, of the input, compute and output phases. This type of program, where performance is dependent on that of the peripherals, is known as *input/output-limited*.

1.4 CPU LIMITED JOBS

There is a second class of program, such as those performing complex scientific calculations, which may do a lot of processing for each card read. Such a situation is illustrated in figure 1.4.

This type of job is known as *CPU-limited*, as the speed of the CPU is the

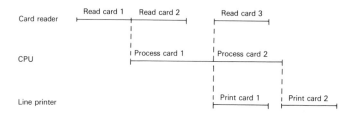

Figure 1.4 Process sequence for CPU-limited system

dominant factor in determining the total run time of the program. In a simple system, the CPU efficiency when running this type of program is, of course, very high (≈ 100 per cent), although it is now the peripherals that are being under utilised. This again is not particularly cost-effective. Running computer systems in such a simple way is, in general, very wasteful of the resources available to a program.

1.5 SUMMARY

The simple systems just described illustrate the extremes of input/output-limited and CPU-limited jobs, presupposing that each job could be put into either classification. Not only is it impossible for a computer to predetermine the type of jobs before execution, but also during execution the constraining limitations of any particular program will probably change. Consider, for example, a scientific program that initially reads a lot of data and so is input/output-limited, then performs a lengthy computation when it is CPU-limited and finally prints out the results and is again input/output-limited. Ideally we would like a system that makes the optimum use of *all* the resources available within the computer system.

So far we have assumed that it is always desirable to have an operating system to control the running of the computer. However, there are some applications where this is impractical. The operating system inevitably consumes some resources itself (for example, store, CPU time). In situations such as certain process-control applications, the result of putting an operating system between the application program and the process that it is controlling may be unacceptable. It may be more important that the application program reacts instantaneously to an external stimulus, irrespective of any efficiency considerations, and thus an operating system such as is found on a large multi-user computer system would be a disadvantage. Although this type of application may have an underlying 'system', which may have some of the attributes of other operating systems, its design is usually rather specialised;

accordingly it will not be considered further in this book. Instead we shall concentrate on the broad principles behind the design of a simple, general-purpose operating system.

1.6 REFERENCES

D. H. R. Huxtable and J. M. M. Pinkerton (1977). 'The Hardware/Software Interface of the ICL 2900 Range of Computers', *Computer Journal*, Vol. 20, pp. 290-5.

J. L. Keedy (1976). 'The Management and Technological Approach to the Design of System B', *Proc. 7th Australian Computer Conf.*, Perth, pp. 997-1013.

D. M. Ritchie and K. Thompson (1974). 'The UNIX Time-sharing System', *Communications of the ACM*, Vol. 17, pp. 365-75.

1.7 PROBLEMS

1. Describe the features which make a basic operating system useful.

2. How can the operating system affect the users' view of a computer?

3. Discuss the relative significance of CPU-limited and input/output-limited jobs.

2 Performance of Input/Output Systems

An essential requirement of any computer system is its ability to communicate with the user by means of input/output (I/O) devices. However, as shown in chapter 1, the overall performance of the computer system is very dependent on the behaviour of the input/output peripherals. We considered the performance of individual jobs that may be input/output-limited or CPU-limited. However, in general, computer systems must be able to run a variety of jobs and the aim must be to achieve good utilisation of all the systems' resources under the various conditions. Effective techniques for controlling the peripheral operations are therefore needed.

This chapter considers some of the features and techniques that are used in peripheral management to improve the utilisation of input/output devices. It must be emphasised that the concepts described here, namely multiprogramming, interrupts and buffering, are not solely features of the input/output system, although it is in this area that they have proved to be most effective.

2.1 SIMPLE PRINCIPLES OF MULTIPROGRAMMING

If we were to examine the mix of jobs running on a machine over a period of time, it would probably be found that some jobs were input/output-limited and required very little computing time, whereas others were CPU-limited and performed only a very small number of input/output operations. If it were possible to mix jobs of these types together, then it might be possible to achieve good performance of both the CPU and peripherals.

At the simplest level, arrangements might be made to multiprogram a CPU-limited and an input/output-limited job, keeping both in the store together. The input/output-limited job would then be run until it had to wait for a transfer to be completed. At that point, the CPU-limited job would be scheduled to use up the spare processing capacity. When the peripheral transfer had been completed, a switch back to the input/output-limited job would be made. This processing sequence is illustrated in figure 2.1.

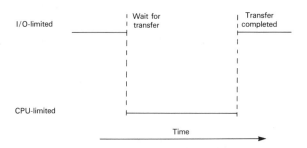

Figure 2.1 Process sequence for simple multiprogramming

The concept of multiprogramming a series of jobs is straightforward; however it is not always possible to have prior knowledge of whether a job is CPU-limited or input/output-limited. Also a job may well change between these two states during its execution; for example, a scientific program which is normally CPU-limited while performing calculations may be input/output-limited when reading its data or printing its results.

The technique of multiprogramming to improve performance suffers from one major disadvantage, that is that CPU limited jobs will inevitably need to perform some input/output operations during the course of running. Clearly the same set of peripherals cannot be used by more than one job in the machine, or the input and output of the jobs would be unacceptably interleaved. Extra peripherals would therefore be needed for this scheme to work effectively.

2.2 THE USE OF INTERRUPTS

In a system that is multiprogramming a number of jobs, the most difficult problem in controlling the peripherals is to determine when a peripheral transfer has been completed. The simplest technique is periodically to examine the control registers associated with a device, but this can be very time-consuming and therefore extremely wasteful, since this time could be used for other more useful operations.

The *interrupt* mechanism is designed to overcome this problem. With this scheme, all peripherals have a special control signal into the CPU. When a device finishes a transfer, such as when an input device has a character available or an output device has printed a character, the peripheral issues this control signal, so telling the CPU hardware that the transfer has been completed. The action of the CPU in servicing this interrupt is to stop obeying the current sequence of instructions, dump sufficient registers to enable the current process to be restarted after the device has been serviced and jump to an 'interrupt routine'. Within this routine, the status of the device is examined and appropriate actions taken to service the device. Other processes in the machine may be activated within this routine and scheduled. If we return from this interrupt routine back to the program that was running when the interrupt occurred, the registers dumped at the time of the interrupt can be reloaded, and the program resumed as if the interrupt had not occurred.

An interrupt mechanism is essential if effective multiprogramming of input/output-limited and CPU-limited jobs is to be achieved. Thus, the input/output-limited job controls the peripherals, halting while the device is in transfer, and the occurrence of an interrupt is the signal to switch back to it from the CPU-limited job when the transfer has been completed.

2.3 THE CONCEPT OF BUFFERING

In chapter 1 the driving of peripherals and the effect on CPU efficiency was briefly examined. For the most simple scheme the time taken to process a character was:

input time + process time + output time

which in our example averaged at

(200 + 10 + 200) ms per line

This performance was improved by overlapping some of the operations, in that case by reading the next character before it was actually required. The processing rate was then determined by the slowest operation and was given by

Max(input time, process time, output time)

or 200 ms in the example

As mentioned in the earlier section on multiprogramming, programs, of course, do not perform input, output and processing at such a nice orderly rate and there may be long periods when the program is computing without performing input/output operations. It would be better to keep the peripherals busy all the time, even through these periods. Basically, an even flow of characters to and from the peripherals is desirable, even though the program might be consuming the input characters at a very uneven rate and producing the output characters at an equally irregular rate.

The solution, in computing terms, is to use a reservoir or buffer to smooth out the discrepancies between supply and demand. Typically, a complete line of input might be accumulated in the store before it is actually needed. When the program requires the line, it can process it at the store speed rather than the peripheral speed.

Notice, however, that the actual run time for a given program is still given by

$$\text{Max(input time, process time, output time)}$$

although, in this case, we are considering the processing of complete lines of input rather than individual characters.

It is also worth noting that if the jobs are either very input/output-limited or CPU-limited (that is, input time $\gg$ process time or process time $\gg$ input time) then the run time is not altered significantly by overlapping, since

$$\text{Max(input/output time, process time)} \simeq \text{input/output time} + \text{process time}$$

2.4 IMPLEMENTATION OF A SIMPLE BUFFERING SYSTEM

Consider a very simple buffering system for a device, such as a card reader or paper tape reader; it can be seen that two activites are involved:

> the buffering process   (the producer)
> the user process   (the consumer)

From the point of view of the buffering system, the two processes can be regarded as operating in parallel, so performing the following sequences:

Buffering
```
REPEAT
    read a character from the device
    place it in the buffer
FOREVER
```

User
```
REPEAT
    read a character
    perform some (random) amount of computing
UNTIL end of input
```

In the user process, the only activity that is of interest to the buffering system is the 'read a character' operation. No assumptions can be made about the rest of the user job as the user is free to change it at any time and in any way he wishes. A procedure INSYM could therefore be introduced to form the user's interface with the buffering system.

These simple sequences are not particularly informative, so it is necessary to expand these operations to the level at which code could be generated. This gives:

Buffering process

```
REPEAT
    (read a character from the device)
    WHILE reader state ◊ 'done' DO
        BEGIN
            start reader ·
            REPEAT (nothing)
            UNTIL reader state = 'done'
                OR reader state = 'error'
        END

    (place it in the buffer)
    buffer [bufptr] : = character
    bufptr : = bufptr + 1
    IF character = 'newline' THEN
        BEGIN
            wake user process if halted
            wait for user process to empty buffer
            bufptr : = 1
        END
FOREVER
```

User process (insym procedure)

```
WHILE buffer empty DO (nothing)
character : = buffer [userptr]
userptr : = userptr + 1
IF character = 'newline' THEN
    BEGIN
        inform buffering process that buffer is empty
        userptr : = 1
    END
```

This sequence, which uses an area of store (buffer) and two pointers to it (bufptr and userptr) leaves several unresolved points:

(1) In the buffering process, how is it possible to 'REPEAT (nothing) UNTIL reader state = 'done' OR reader state = 'error''? (The reader has read a character or failed.)

The buffering process is, in practice, an interrupt routine, so having started the device the action required is just to wait until the next interrupt occurs.

(2) How is it possible to 'wake user process if halted'?

This can be done by setting a flag to say that information is in the buffer. The user process then has to test the flag before trying to read characters from the buffer.

(3) How is it possible to 'wait for user process to empty buffer'?

One solution is not to bother trying to restart the reader again, but to let the user process restart it when the buffer is empty. The resultant interrupt will have the effect of restarting the buffering process.

Such a modified sequence now becomes:

interrupt:

```
WHILE reader state <> done DO
    BEGIN
        start reader
        wait for done/error (return from interrupt)
    END

buffer [bufptr] := character
bufptr := bufptr + 1
IF character = newline THEN
    BEGIN
        wake user process
        bufptr := 1
        stop reader (inhibit interrupts)
        wait for user to empty buffer
    END
```

insym:

```
WHILE buffer is empty DO (nothing)
character := buffer [userptr]
userptr := userptr + 1
IF character = newline then
    BEGIN
        set 'buffer empty' flag
        restart buffering process
        userptr := 1
    END
```

There are some quite obvious deficiencies with this code sequence. For example, there is no check on the length of line so a very long line could cause an access to be made beyond the space allocated for the buffer. The treatment of errors is also very crude, since restarting a device when it is in error (for example, with no cards or paper tape in it) will again cause an immediate interrupt if the error condition still holds. However, it shows that, in principle, buffering systems are quite simple and straightforward to implement.

2.5 SUMMARY

Improved utilisation of a simple computer system can be achieved by the techniques of multiprogramming and the buffering of input and output characters. Such a system requires the use of interrupts for it to be effective.

   We have considered a simple buffering system to illustrate the concepts that can be used. This is at best a simplistic overview and great care is required in the detailed coding of the system. The indeterminate nature of peripheral interrupts frequently causes problems in the operation of system software. For example, consider the sequences:

User program	Interrupt routine
read flag	set flag
IF flag set THEN	return from interrupt
perform some action	
ELSE	
wait for interrupt	

   Accessing shared variables, such as 'flag', needs special care as interrupts can occur at any time during the normal sequencing of instructions. In this example, if an interrupt were to occur after the user program had read the flag but before meeting the wait instruction, the user program would find itself (1) with the flag set (but not noticed), (2) waiting for an interrupt that had already occurred.

This is fairly typical of the interlock conditions that have to be taken into account when writing system software and reflects the indeterminate nature of operating systems. Although it is quite likely an interrupt would *not* occur at that point, inevitably one will occur at some time. The net effect is that the program fails in a manner that is not entirely reproduceable (as it is too dependent on the tolerance of mechanical devices). Techniques for resolving this type of problem will be considered later.

2.6 PROBLEMS

1. What is the motivation for multiprogramming? Describe the

characteristics of programs which make multiprogramming a desirable feature.

2. What is buffering and what are its limitations?

3. How might interrupts be used so as to prevent programs in infinite loops from running indefinitely.

4. Explain why interrupts are important in a system which supports parallel activities.

3 Spooling

It has been shown that the performance of a computer system deteriorates significantly when a user program drives the input and output peripherals directly. This deterioration is, of course, dependent on the extent to which a program is performing input/output operations, but a program that spends most of its time waiting for the completion of peripheral transfers will obviously be using the CPU usefully for very little of the time. In early systems, the CPU was the most expensive commodity and so attempts at improving the CPU efficiency were the main stimulus behind the development of operating systems. To some extent, therefore, the historical development of operating systems reflects the techniques used to improve the performance.

3.1 OFFLINE SPOOLING

The disparity in speed between the early CPUs and the conventional peripherals, such as card readers and lineprinters, was the major reason for poor performance, particularly for input/output-limited jobs. The solution initially adopted was to reduce this discrepancy by using only fast peripherals on the main CPU. This technique is epitomised by the IBM systems in the early 1960s which used magnetic tapes as the input and output media on the main CPU.

In the early offline spooling systems, jobs and their associated data were loaded on to tape using slow, comparatively inexpensive processors. When a batch of jobs had been formed on the tape, the tape was transferred to the main CPU where the jobs and data were read and processed at a relatively fast speed. In a similar way, output from the jobs was written to tape on the main CPU and this was later transferred to the slower processor for printing. This offline spooling system is illustrated in figure 3.1.

This system had a number of advantages over its simple predecessors, namely

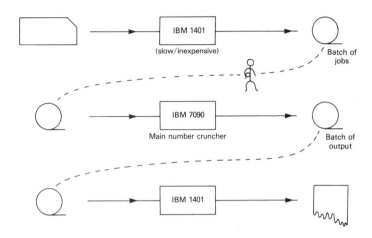

Figure 3.1 Offline spooling system

(1) Improved efficiency.
The main processor had a high input/output rate because of the speed of the magnetic tapes. The performance was therefore improved, even for input/output–limited jobs. The slow processors dedicated to servicing the batch peripherals were more closely matched to the speed of the devices and so their efficiency was quite reasonable. The low cost of these processors also made any inefficiency more tolerable.

(2) Simplified operating procedures.
Performing input/output operations on the main processor were considerably simplified, as the only type of peripheral on this machine was magnetic tape. The reading and writing of blocks to tape is a far more simple task than driving a variety of peripherals, like card readers or lineprinters, which exhibit vastly differing characteristics.

(3) Convenience for remote users.
It was possible for remote users to have their own slow processor for spooling their jobs on tape. The

transfer of tapes to the main machine was far more
convenient than, for example, transferring boxes of
punched cards which might be dropped and shuffled.

Although these advantages made the system far more attractive, it did
still have drawbacks, most notably the following:

(1) Long turnaround time.
     The time to create a tape with a batch of jobs, run
     the whole tape through the main processor and print
     all the output for all the jobs was often quite
     lengthy. This was particularly unfortunate for jobs
     doing few input/output operations. For example, the
     sequence for running jobs might be

```
 |               |              |              |            |
 |cards -> tape|run all jobs on tape|tape -> printer|
 |   2 hours   |    2 hours.   |    2 hours   |
 |             |               |              |            |
```

(2) No priority or online access.
     The only way of achieving priority access was to take
     a magnetic tape containing the priority job to the
     main processor and run it as soon as the processor
     became free. Even then it might be several hours
     before the jobs currently being read from tape were
     fully processed.

(3) Additional hardware required.
     In addition to the extra processors for driving the
     peripherals, there was also quite a lot of extra
     expense for the magnetic tape drives.

For these reasons, offline spooling is now rarely used, although a
similar technique is sometimes used for commercial data preparation.
Here 'key to tape' or 'key to disc' systems form the data on fast media
for subsequent input to larger transaction-processing systems.

3.2 ONLINE SPOOLING

The problems of offline spooling are, to some extent, solved by the
online spooling system illustrated in figure 3.2.

In this system, only a single processor is used and a rudimentary
spooling system co-exists in the processor with a user job. The
operating system is multiprogrammed with the user job and transfers data
between the slow input/output devices and the backing store (disc). The
user job performs its input/output operations to and from the backing
store and thus exhibits the same characteristics as in the offline spooling

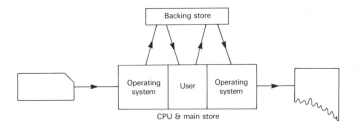

Figure 3.2 Simple online spooling system

system, where the input/output transfers operate at a fast rate.

To some extent, this situation is analogous to the simple multiprogramming case considered in chapter 2. Here the operating system is the input/output-limited process and the user job is the CPU-limited one. Unlike the simple case, however, the user job never needs to drive the slow devices as all its input/output operations are on documents held on the disc. The timing sequence for this simple multiprogramming case is shown in figure 3.3.

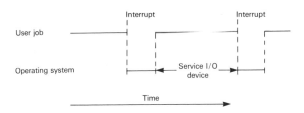

Figure 3.3 Multiprogramming of the operating system with a user job

The passage of a job through this simple spooling system begins by loading a deck of cards containing details of the job into the card reader. The operating system drives this device, so putting the characters read by the card reader into a buffer in main memory. As disc drives are unable to transfer individual characters, the size of this buffer must correspond to the size of the data blocks held on the disc. When sufficient cards have been read to fill the buffer, it is transferred to the disc and the operation is repeated. Thus, a complete deck of cards might appear on the disc as a number of blocks of characters, which together form a complete input document.

When the user program is run, the input document is brought into store one block at a time. When the user calls a procedure to read a character, individual characters are extracted from this block and returned to the user program. When the block is empty, a disc transfer is started to bring the next block from the disc. The user program thus performs its input operations at disc speed rather than at the speed of the card reader.

A similar sequence operates (in reverse) to form output documents on the disc. These are subsequently brought back into memory by the operating system and printed on the lineprinter. This is illustrated in figure 3.4.

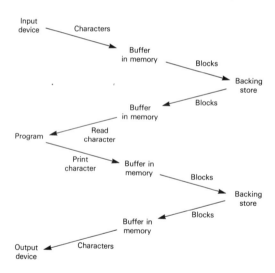

Figure 3.4 Passage of a job through a simple spooling system

As with the offline spooling system, this system has many advantages over the simple example where peripherals are controlled directly by user programs; most notably these are as follows:

(1) Efficient CPU usage.
As with the offline spooling system, input/output operations within the user programs are performed using a fast device (the disc) and thus they run efficiently. The operating system drives the slow peripherals using interrupts, and so this is also efficient in terms of CPU usage.

(2) Efficient peripheral usage.
Building up queues of input and output documents on the disc has a smoothing effect, so that input/output operations can be performed for input/output-limited jobs while running CPU-limited jobs.

(3) Fast turnaround.
In contrast with offline spooling, it is not essential to wait for complete input tapes or output tapes to be formed before jobs are run or the output printed.

(4) Priority access.
As discs are random access devices, if there is a backlog of jobs waiting to be processed they can be taken out of sequence and the most urgent given priority access to the machine.

(5) Multiple input/output documents.
As user programs are processing input/output documents held on the disc, an actual peripheral device no longer has to be associated with an input/output document. Thus, it is possible to have multiple input/output documents for a job, even though the computer system has only a single card reader/lineprinter. This would be impractical if the documents were not buffered on the disc. An extension of this scheme allows some documents to remain on the disc between successive runs of a user's program. These 'permanent documents' are, in effect, files.

3.3 DESIGN OF A SIMPLE SPOOLING SYSTEM

The remainder of this chapter considers in detail the design of an operating system that could be used for online spooling. Within the operating system, certain essential functions can be identified, and so the following components might be required:

(1) INPUT SYSTEM   Drives the card reader and forms complete input documents on the disc.

(2) OUTPUT SYSTEM   Drives the lineprinter, using output documents on the disc.

(3) JOB SCHEDULER   Chooses which of the jobs on the disc is to be run next.

(4) JOB PROCESSOR   Runs the user job, arranging to call the correct compilers/assemblers into store, and provides routines to perform input and output operations for the user job.

(5) OUTPUT SCHEDULER   Chooses which of the output documents queued on the disc is to be printed next. (Allows documents for priority jobs to jump the queue.)

(6) DISC MANAGER   Coordinates use of the disc, since all other components use the disc.

It is convenient to regard each of these as completely asynchronous operations, or processes. They are not independent, however, as there must be interactions between the various components of this operating system. Figure 3.5 shows the structure of the system:

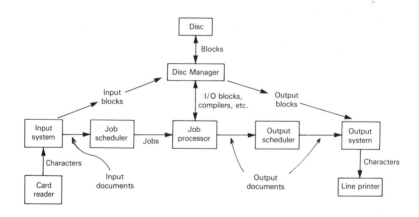

Figure 3.5 Processes in a simple online spooling operating system

3.3.1 Input System

This is synchronised to the operation of the card reader. The characters read by the card reader are packed into blocks and, when the blocks are full, the disc manager writes them to the disc. At the end of each input document, information about the document (such as the location on the disc, the priority, job name or user name) are passed to the job scheduler.

```
REPEAT
    start card reader              {interrupt routine reads complete  }
                                   {cards into an 80-byte buffer, then}
                                   {frees input spooler               }
    wait                           {for card to be read               }
    IF control card THEN           {pass details directly to job      }
        save details in job list   {scheduler, via the job list       }
    ELSE
        BEGIN
        copy card to main buffer   {as the disc needs large blocks    }
        IF buffer full THEN        {write block to disc               }
            BEGIN
            allocate space on disc {by calling on the disc manager    }
            record disc address
            make entry on disc transfer queue
            free (disc manager)    {to perform the transfer           }
            wait                   {for transfer to complete          }
            END
        END
    IF end of document THEN
        BEGIN
        mark document in job list  {for the job scheduler             }
        wake (job scheduler)
        END
FOREVER
```

3.3.2 Job Scheduler

The job scheduler keeps a list of all the jobs in the machine and information about the input documents required by the jobs.

Note that jobs can have more than one input and one output document, even though only one card reader and one lineprinter is available. For example, there might be one input document containing the program and another holding the data. The job scheduler can start the job only when all its input documents are available, so when a job is submitted to the machine the number of input and output documents required by the job must be stated. This normally appears as a job description which may be submitted as a separate document. The program data documents have information on their first card to identify the job with which they are associated.

```
REPEAT
    WHILE job processor is busy OR job list empty DO wait
    select a job from the job list
    set 'current job' = this job
    free (job processor)
FOREVER
```

3.3.3 Job Processor

The job processor is told which job to run next by the job scheduler. This involves passing information about the location of a job and its associated input documents on the disc. The job processor also knows the location on the disc of all the compilers and other system software.

When the program is being run by the job processor it outputs characters, which are collected in a buffer in store. This action is very similar to the input system in that blocks of characters are eventually transferred to the disc to form complete output documents. The job processor also passes information about the location (and priority) of the output documents to the output scheduler.

```
REPEAT
    IF 'current job' empty THEN wait   {for job scheduler to supply a job}
    read compiler name from input      {using INCH                       }
        document
    make entry on disc transfer queue  {to fetch compiler to memory      }
    free (disc manager)                {to perform the transfer          }
    wait                               {for transfer to complete         }
    jump to compiler entry

                                       {user program executes . . .      }
                                       {and returns by calling stop       }

stop:
    set 'current job' to empty
    release any unread blocks of input
    call outch(0) until last block
        has been written to disc
    make entry in output document list
    free (output scheduler)            {another document available       }
    free (job scheduler)               {request another job to run       }
FOREVER
```

Inch and Outch Routines

```
inch:
    IF input buffer empty THEN
       BEGIN
       release previous input block (if any)
       make entry in disc transfer queue to
          read next input block
       free (disc manager)              {to perform disc transfer}
       wait                             {for transfer to complete}
       set buffer pointer to start of input buffer
       END
    take 1 character from buffer
    RETURN


outch:
    write 1 character to output buffer
    IF buffer full THEN
       BEGIN
       allocate disc block and record its address
       make entry in disc transfer queue to
          write output buffer to disc
       free (disc manager)              {to perform disc transfer}
       wait                             {for transfer to complete}
       set buffer pointers to start of output buffer
       END
    RETURN
```

3.3.4 Output Scheduler

The output scheduler maintains a list of documents to be printed. When the lineprinter is free, the output scheduler selects the document to be printed next and tells the output system the location of the document on the disc.

```
    REPEAT
       WHILE lineprinter busy OR output list empty wait
       select a document from the output list
       set 'current output document' for the output system
       free (output system)
    FOREVER
```

3.3.5 Output System

The output system retrieves blocks of characters from the disc and drives the lineprinter (either a character at a time or a line at a time).

```
REPEAT
   IF 'current output document' empty THEN wait
   REPEAT
      get disc address of next output block
      make entry in disc transfer queue to
         transfer output block to core
      free (disc manager)      {to perform disc transfer       }
      wait                     {for transfer to complete       }
      start printer            {the interrupt routine can output}
                               {a complete block, then free the }
                               {output spooler                  }
      REPEAT wait              {for block to be output          }
      UNTIL block has been output
      release disc space occupied by the block
   UNTIL end of document
FOREVER
```

3.3.6 Disc Manager

The interface between the disc manager and the other processes in the system is at a fairly simple level. The main functions required of the disc manager are:

(1) read a block from the disc
(2) write a block to the disc
(3) allocate a free block on the disc
(4) return a block to the pool of free space on the disc

```
REPEAT
   IF disc transfer queue empty THEN wait
   select a transfer request from the queue
   start disc transfer      {the interrupt routine will  }
                            {simply free the disc manager}
                            {when the transfer completes }
   REPEAT wait              {for transfer complete       }
   UNTIL transfer is completed
   free (process which requested the transfer)
FOREVER
```

3.3.7 The Coordinator

There is one component of our system that does not appear in figure 3.5 and is not directly concerned with processing user jobs. However, it is essential for the running of operating–system processes. It is called the *coordinator* and is responsible for scheduling the system processes and providing suitable synchronisation operations. These operations can be provided by two procedures:

(1) WAIT halts the current process and re-enters the scheduler.
(2) FREE makes the specified process available for scheduling.

```
coordinator:

    REPEAT
        p := 0                          (Initialise circular scan of processes)
        REPEAT
            IF process(p) free THEN     (Find a process to run              )
               BEGIN
               current proc := p
               restore registers for the process
                   and reenter process

                                        (Process P executes . . .           )
                                        (and exits by calling wait           )

wait:
               save registers
               mark process no longer free
               END
            p := p+1
        UNTIL p > max process number
    FOREVER


free:                                   (Free process (proc)                )
    mark process (proc) as free
    IF current process = job process THEN
        BEGIN
        save registers                  (Enter coordinator to choose a system )
        enter coordinator               (process in preference to the user job)
        END
```

3.4 PROBLEMS

1. What is spooling? Compare and contrast online and offline spooling.

2. The table below gives the input, compute and output times for three jobs submitted to a spooling system:

	Job 1	Job 2	Job 3
Input	5	2	5
Compute	4	2	3
Output	1	3	2

(a) What sequence of processing the three jobs minimises the total time to run the three, assuming that the order of input determines the order of processing and the order of output?

(b) Can the order of (a) be improved on if the jobs may be processed and output in a sequence other than the one in which they are input? If so, how?

(c) What is the best that can possibly be achieved if the jobs are input in the order job 1, job 2, job 3? (The system does not usually have control over the order of input.)

(d) Answer the above three questions with the criterion of minimising the average turnaround time for the batch of jobs.

3. Describe the structure of a simple spooling system and the operation of each process in this system. How might this system be extended to provide multi-access facilities? Describe the changes and the additional processes required.

4. Describe the advantages of a spooling system over one in which input and output are buffered directly between a program and the peripheral. What buffering techniques might be used within a simple operating system running just batch jobs? Explain how the passage of a job through the machine is helped by buffering.

4 Time-Sharing Systems

The simple spooling system considered in chapter 3 is fairly restricted in its applications. Its mode of working, where single jobs or batches of jobs are submitted to the machine and a job is started only when the previous one has been completed, is very effective in achieving good utilisation of the computer system. However, it is not particularly convenient from the user's point of view. The ability to interact with a program is both desirable when developing software and essential for certain types of applications, yet this facility is not available with the spooling system. Thus, a more common type of operating system is the *multi-access* or *time-sharing* system, where many users are (apparently) able to make simultaneous use of the computer.

4.1 CHARACTERISTICS OF THE TIME-SHARING SYSTEM

The most important characteristic of a multi-access system is that the computer is reacting to stimuli from a number of devices connected to the machine. The devices may be terminals and the stimulus may be provided by a user typing on the keyboard. However, this is not always the case and, in general, the precise nature of the devices and the ways in which the computer responds are dependent on the application for which the system was designed. It is possible to classify multi-access systems according to their application, which gives three main types of system.

(1) Real time systems

The main use of real time systems is to support some type of process-control application. The important characteristic of real-time systems is that any interaction with the computer must receive a response within a predefined time period. It is essential that this response time can be guaranteed. (Consider the implications of poor response from a system that is controlling an aircraft or the processing in a chemical plant.) This requirement usually means that the software is special purpose and dedicated to one particular application. The peripherals on such a system are also likely to be special, being sensing devices operating with analogue signals rather than conventional terminals.

(2) Special-purpose, transaction-processing systems

A typical example of this type of system is that used for airline reservations. Here the users are interacting with predefined packages, either for the input of transactions or the interrogation of a central database. The types of interactions are thus fairly limited. Once again, the system must ensure that the response time is reasonable (particularly if the airline wishes to keep its potential customers satisfied). However, the response requirements are not as critical as for the real-time system.

(3) General-purpose time-sharing systems

This might be regarded as the normal type of computer system, where users are able to develop and interact with programs online. The level of facilities provided by this type of system can vary considerably, but in all cases, it is much more convenient for the users than the simple spooling system.

Even in its most primitive form, where the terminal is little more than a personalised input/output device, the psychology of interacting directly with the computer rather than relying on operators makes this a far more amenable system, and an immediate indication of 'silly errors' in control or editing commands ensures a higher productivity for the user. In systems that allow much more interaction, the user may be able to stop and restart his executing program, set break points, inspect and change variables or step through the program. (Compare this with the facilities provided for the sole user of a machine interacting via the operator's front panel of the computer.) Again, the emphasis here is on the productivity of the user, in that good facilities for developing new software are provided rather than optimising the use of machine resources. In general, the provision of this type of facility is very costly in terms of system efficiency.

4.2 DESIGN OF A TIME-SHARING SYSTEM

The design of a general-purpose time-sharing system can largely be based on that of the simple spooling system. Although the system is primarily supporting terminals, facilities may still be provided for printing documents on a lineprinter or inputting a file or job via a card reader or paper tape reader. The input and output spoolers would therefore still be

Included within the design. A typical design of a simple system is
Illustrated in figure 4.1.

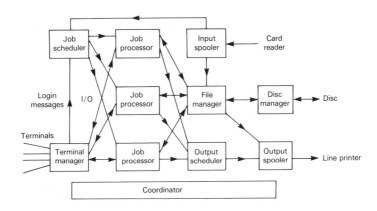

Figure 4.1 Design of a simple time-sharing system

The major feature of this system is that it must be capable of
supporting a number of user jobs that are executed (apparently) at the
same time. Thus, the module responsible for running the user job (that
is, the job processor) has to be replicated for each job in the machine.
The time-sharing option is provided by switching the CPU between these
job processors as each user demands an interaction with his job.
Although effectively there are multiple copies of this job processor
module, and each has its own data space, stack and copies of the
registers, in practice the code provided within each of the job
processors is identical and on some machines a single copy of this code
can be shared. This technique is described in chapter 9.

The other major differences between this system and the simple
spooling system are that facilities must be provided to keep files on the
computer and to drive terminals for input/output. A file system is an
essential requirement of this system as it is no longer feasible to input a
large document via the input device every time a job is run. This was
not the case with the simple spooling system, where large decks of
cards could be submitted on every run of a program. However, it is
clearly impractical for a user sitting at a terminal to do likewise.

Although it would be possible to integrate the functions of a file
manager within the disc manager, logically they are quite different and
so it is better to regard them as being in separate modules of the
system. The disc manager is primarily concerned with allocating space

on the disc and arranging for transfers whereas the file manager is more concerned with the management of file directories, the security of files and any associated accounting.

The input and output spoolers in the system might also make use of the facilities provided by the file manager, rather than by communicating directly with the disc manager. By saving input and output documents as files, unprocessed documents can be retained across machine restarts, thus avoiding the need to resubmit jobs whose output had not been printed when the machine stopped.

The functions of the terminal manager are very different from those of the spoolers that control other input/output devices. Whereas the input spooler buffers a complete job on the disc before passing information about the document to the job scheduler, the terminal manager will be buffering, in main memory, only single characters or single lines of input data. The first line typed by a user will be sent from the terminal manager to the job scheduler. This will normally identify the user and provide any passwords and charging information that may be required as part of the normal sequence for logging in to the system. The job scheduler assigns a job processor to that particular terminal and informs the terminal manager accordingly. All subsequent input and output operations are then made directly between the terminal manager and the job processor.

This simple model of a time-sharing system is the basis for further discussion and elaboration in the second part of this book. During the course of this, the techniques and algorithms used in some of the modules will be described in more detail and new modules may be added to our simple model in order to fulfil the requirements of a powerful, general-purpose time-sharing system.

4.3 PROBLEMS

1. Describe in detail the design of a time sharing system, indicating the main functions of each module and the nature of the communication between modules.

2. Outline the sequence of events within the operating system when a user logs on to the system from a terminal, and types commands to his process.

3. Describe the design of a simple time sharing system that provides interactive file editing, compiling and running of a user's programs. Indicate the main functions of each module. Give a detailed account of the actions inside this operating system in response to a user typing a line of input.

Part 2 Operating System Techniques

5 Buffering Techniques

5.1 MORE SOPHISTICATED BUFFERING TECHNIQUES

In chapter 2 we examined the design of a buffering scheme that might be used for driving peripherals in a simple system to provide more effective use of the input/output devices. This simple scheme has a number of major deficiencies; in particular, there are many occasions when the performance is inadequate. Figure 5.1 shows the operation of our buffering system in precise detail and from this the major problems can be identified.

Notice that there is a short period when the reader is switched off while the user process is taking characters from the buffer. This does not matter too much for the card or paper tape reader except that it increases wear on the mechanical mechanisms used for starting and stopping the reader. Unfortunately, there are certain devices where this delay does matter. Some examples of these are as follows:

(1) Devices that supply data at a continuous rate.
An example of this would be a remote terminal connected to a synchronous line. In this case, the remote terminal determines the transmission rate, and a 'gap' in receiving would mean that data is lost. There is no way of telling the terminal to stop transmitting while the buffer is emptied.

(2) Some magnetic tape drives.
(With magnetic tapes, blocks of data rather than single characters or lines are read. However, the same principles apply.) Data blocks on the tape are separated by a short, interblock gap. Unfortunately with some tape decks the tapes take a while to get up to full speed. Reading a block involves skipping back down the tape for a couple of blocks and then winding forward again so that the tape has reached full speed by the time that the required block is over the read heads. This means that when it is

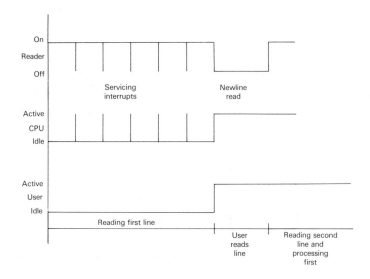

Figure 5.1 Buffering system.

necessary to read consecutive blocks, it is impractical to stop the tape between them. The interblock gap might also be too short to allow the block to be processed and the buffer emptied.

(3) Online terminals.
The delay in processing a line is artificially extended in this case when the user job has to wait for its turn of the CPU. Thus, under heavy loading, the response time might be quite long and during this period the user will not be able to continue typing.

5.2 DOUBLE BUFFERING

A solution to these problems is to use two (or even more) buffers. Thus, after the device has filled one buffer, the user program can be allowed to read from it while the device fills the other, as shown in figure 5.2.

The buffers are used alternately, with buffer 1 being filled while buffer 2 is being emptied, and vice versa. Provided that the processing rate is faster than the input rate (or the rates are approximately equal), the device can be kept operating continuously.

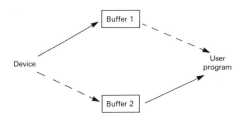

Figure 5.2 Double buffering technique

Before utilising double buffering techniques, some points should be noted:

(1) In a simple system, the processing rate becomes synchronised to the speed of the slowest device and so it is normally only worthwhile to provide double buffering for the slowest device.

(2) It is not worthwhile to provide double buffering if the job that controls the device is CPU-limited.

(3) Double buffering is always worthwhile if it is inconvenient or expensive to stop a device; for example, where loss of characters would otherwise occur.

5.3 CYCLIC (CIRCULAR) BUFFERING

The buffering schemes considered so far try to accumulate the data that the user is going to process in a single burst (for example, one line). The problem with this is that the length of line varies enormously and, if the maximum value is chosen for the size of the buffer, then in most cases space will be wasted.

One solution is to have a single, fairly large buffer that will hold one or more lines. In general, the buffering process will be placing characters into one end of the buffer while the user is removing them from the other. In effect, the user process is 'chasing' the buffering process down the buffer. This is illustrated in figure 5.3 (NL ≡ newline).

When either of the pointers reaches the end of the buffer, it is reset back to the start. There is the obvious danger here that one of the pointers might overtake the other:

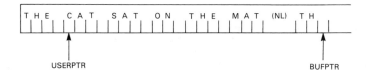

Figure 5.3 Cyclic buffering

If input is faster than processing, BUFPTR might overtake USERPTR, overwriting data that has not yet been read.

If processing is faster than input, USERPTR might overtake BUFPTR and attempt to read data that has not yet been placed in the buffer.

Obviously, these can be overcome by programming certain checks into the buffering procedures.

Terminal handling provides one of the most common applications for the use of cyclic buffering. It also illustrates how more sophisticated facilities can be introduced using basically a very simple scheme.

5.3.1 Requirements

The system used for buffering terminal input has to satisfy the following requirements:

(1) The user process is wakened only when there is a complete line of input for it to process. There is a significant overhead associated with scheduling a process and this is to be avoided as much as possible. The process is therefore only wakened when the user is expecting a response from the system.

(2) The user must be able to type complete lines of input up to the maximum width of, say, 80 characters. This determines the minimum size of the buffer.

(3) The user must also be able to correct typing errors on the current line. This involves looking for a logical 'backspace' character (for example, ←).

(4) The user should be able to type more than one line if the system is too busy to process his input instantly.

(5) The user process must be capable of re-reading the line that it is reading. This enables facilities, such as repeating operations in the editor, to be implemented easily.

(6) A prompt should be output to the user if the system is waiting for input and the user has not started typing the next line.

5.3.2 Implementation

These facilities can be provided using a cyclic buffering system with four pointers, as in figure 5.4.

Figure 5.4 Cyclic buffering for terminal input

The system has the following characteristics:

(1) The buffer is at least 80 characters long (the length of a line).

(2) Characters are inserted by the buffering process at BUFPTR.

(3) Characters are removed by the user process at USERPTR.

(4) The user process is wakened whenever a newline is placed in the buffer.

(5) BUFLIN records the last newline character placed in the buffer. This fulfils two functions:

    (a) The user process is halted as soon as USERPTR reaches BUFLIN. In addition, a prompt will be output if the user has not typed any more input, that is when BUFPTR = BUFLIN.

    (b) The logical backspace facility operates only as far back as BUFLIN. This prevents the user from deleting characters that have already been read by his process.

(6) USERLIN records the last newline character read by the user process. BUFPTR is not allowed to advance past this point, so that the user process is always able to re-read the current line.

5.4 PROBLEMS

1. Draw timing diagrams to illustrate the operation of single and double buffering systems for a program that is:
   (a) input-limited
   (b) output-limited
   (c) CPU-limited
   (d) none of the above.

2. Give reasons for the use of buffering in an operating system. Describe in detail the buffering that might be used in a general-purpose computer system that supports batch and interactive peripherals, discs, communication lines and magnetic tapes.

6 Scheduling – Principles

The organisation of the operating system developed so far allows for the time-sharing of the CPU between a number of processes. This technique, however, poses a number of problems; most notably, sharing the available resources between the different job processors. The allocation of resources is one of the most significant problems faced by an operating system. In this chapter, we shall examine the problems of allocating CPU time between the different processes, and some of the basic principles involved in job scheduling.

The main objective of job scheduling is to allocate CPU time to the various jobs in such a way as to optimise some aspect of system performance. The main items we are interested in are:

(1) to provide a good response/turnaround time
(2) to meet user specified deadlines
(3) to provide a high CPU utilisation
(4) to provide good utilisation of other system resources

To some extent these are interrelated, with the effect that optimising one of them might degrade the performance of the system with respect to the others. For example, providing a good response time at a terminal will inevitably incur some system overheads, with the effect that overall CPU utilisation is reduced. Thus, scheduling involves a compromise between the various objectives, and the emphasis on each is naturally dependent on the precise nature and use of the system.

6.1 PREEMPTIVE AND NON-PREEMPTIVE SCHEDULING

Figure 6.1 outlines the time-sharing system that forms the basis of the system organisation developed so far.

In keeping with the onion model of an operating system, several levels of scheduling are expected within the system, and so far two have

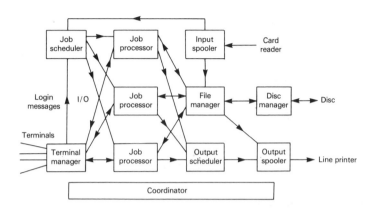

Figure 6.1 Design of a time—sharing system

been identified: (a) the job scheduler and (b) the coordinator. At the higher level, the job scheduler makes a decision as to which user jobs should be allocated a job processor. It will base its decision on factors such as priority, whether a batch job has all its input documents available, whether the user submitting the job has already used up too much computing time in any particular week and whether the user has specified any other scheduling advice (for example, run before midnight, run at weekend). Once a user at a terminal or a job submitted via the input spooler has been assigned to a job processor, the job scheduler relinquishes all control over the job and scheduling decisions are then performed by the coordinator.

Now consider the function of the coordinator in the simple batch system. The coordinator selects a process to enter, loads the registers for that process and, in consequence, re-enters the process. This process is run until it waits for an event (such as a disc transfer).

As there is a certain amount of interaction between processes, a facility must be provided so that one process can free another to perform a task for it. This can be achieved with the 'free' procedure in the coordinator, which removes the halted status from the specified process.

The processes are broadly ordered on priority, so that process(0) is the highest priority and is the first to be examined by the coordinator. However, priority ordering is only applicable in the selection of a process to run. Once it is running, the process is allowed to run to completion (until it calls the WAIT procedure). This is a policy known as *non-preemptive scheduling* and the effect is that, even if a higher priority coordinator:

```
REPEAT
    p := 0                      {Initialise circular scan of processes}
    REPEAT                      {Find a process to run               }
        IF process(p) free THEN
            BEGIN
            current proc := p
            restore registers for the process
            and reenter process

                                {Process P executes . . .            }
                                {and exits by calling  wait          }
wait:
            save registers
            mark process no longer free
            END
        p := p+1
    UNTIL p > max process number
FOREVER
```

process is freed, it will not run until the current process has decided to wait.

This policy is acceptable if the processes return control to the coordinator within a reasonable period of time. However, when a user job is involved this cannot be guaranteed and so the coordinator needs to take special action when considering the user job. Thus, in the free procedure, if it is the job processor that is currently running when a process is freed (where the new process, by definition must be of a higher priority), then the job processor is suspended and the coordinator entered. This is a policy known as *preemptive scheduling*.

6.2 TIME-SLICING

Additional problems occur in time-sharing systems because there are several job processors and each must have the opportunity to use the CPU within the space of a few seconds. The response for a user at a terminal will be unacceptable if a job is waiting much longer than this for a chance to run. Effectively, this means that a user job performing a lot of computing must be *preempted* (that is, have the CPU taken away from it) every few milliseconds to allow other jobs to perform some processing. By this means a job servicing a trivial interaction will receive a rapid response, and jobs performing a lot of computing are, of necessity, delayed to let the short jobs through.

In order to achieve this type of effect, we need:

(1) Some kind of interrupting clock to trigger the system into making scheduling decisions.

(2) Dynamic adjustment of the priority of jobs, so that when a job has had a certain amount of CPU time, other jobs are given preference.

This process of deliberately switching from one process to another on a timed basis is known as *time slicing*. (The quantum of CPU time allocated to the job is, naturally, known as a *time slice*.)

The act of time slicing might be performed by the coordinator, although it is probably better to introduce a new module called the process scheduler (or middle-level scheduler) which dynamically adjusts the priorities used by the coordinator. This is done on each timer interrupt. Providing a new module is advantageous for two reasons:

(1) It avoids complicating the coordinator and, as this is the lowest level scheduler, it is advantageous to keep this as small and efficient as possible.

(2) It enables different kinds of process to be treated differently. For example, some job processors might be processing batch jobs and be exempted from the time slicing discipline.

Effectively, there are now three levels of scheduling:

High-level scheduler	– Job scheduler	Decides which jobs enter the system
Middle-level scheduler	– Process scheduler	Adjusts the priority of processes and organises time slicing
Low-level scheduler	– Coordinator	Performs logical synchronisation of the processes

Each scheduler has a different perspective of how a job passes through the system. The three schedulers that we have now considered are illustrated in figure 6.2.

The use of time slices and the techniques of scheduling so far discussed illustrate how essential preemption is in an online system. However, preemptive scheduling can be worthwhile even in a purely batch system. For example, suppose there are two job processors, a high-priority one for short jobs and a low-priority one for long jobs. It is then advantageous to preempt the long jobs in order to get the short jobs through quickly. Consider a system that is mainly running 10-minute jobs although there are some 10-second jobs as well, under a non-preemptive scheduling discipline, the response for short jobs would

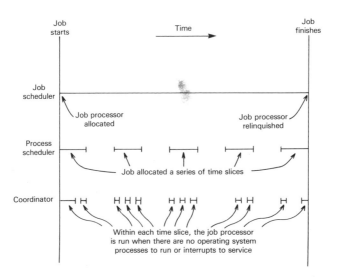

Figure 6.2 Operation of the three schedulers

be around 5 minutes (the average time to complete the current long job). With preemptive scheduling, the short job would be run first and processed in 10 seconds, while the delay for the long job is not significant unless the number of short jobs is high.

The technique of preemption seeks to provide a better response for the users but it is achieved at some cost in terms of overheads associated with the technique. These overheads are:

(1) The processor time consumed by the system when changing between processes.
(2) The space overheads. With a preemptive system, it is necessary to have a sufficient store to hold all the jobs that are currently in a state of execution. A simple 'one job at a time' system naturally requires less store.

Thus, although time slicing might improve the response and turnaround times, it might be at the cost of CPU and other resource utilisations.

6.3 CHOICE OF A TIME SLICE PERIOD

The choice of a value for the time slice given to the job processors is affected by many factors. The most important is probably the way it affects the response time of the system.

Worst response for a *trivial* request = N * time slice

where N is the number of processes requiring time (which must be less than the number of users).

For trivial requests, for example, to input one line, a response of less than 1 or 2 seconds would be expected. For larger tasks, such as compiling, much longer responses are acceptable. This obviously determines the upper bound of our time slice.

The lower bound is determined by two factors:

(1) The overheads of process changing. Transferring jobs to and from store, register dumping and other coordinator actions all cost time, and the quantum allocated for a time slice should not be so small that these overheads dominate the overall performance.

(2) The quantum should be slightly greater than the time required for a 'typical' interaction. If it is less, then every job will require at least two time slices. For example, consider the case where a typical interaction requires a time of t, and a relatively large value has been assigned for the time slice period s. Then when a user is allocated a time slice to perform an interaction, the response time seen by the user is as shown in figure 6.3.

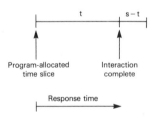

Figure 6.3 Effect of time slice greater than typical interaction

In such a situation, an amount of CPU time equal to (s − t) remains unused from the time slice after the particular interaction has been completed.

On the other hand if the time slice period s has a short value that is less than the typical interaction time t, then the response time seen by the user is as shown in figure 6.4.

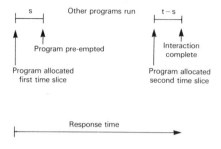

Figure 6.4 Effect of time slice less than typical interaction

The first time slice allocated to the user is not sufficient to complete the interaction and so the user process runs for all that particular time slice. The user program is then preempted and other programs run until the process scheduler allocates a further time slice to this user. In the subsequent interval the user interaction is completed, but it can be seen that the response time for the user has been increased.

In deciding upon a time slice period, a value must be chosen that is at least adequate for servicing a typical user interaction.

6.4 ESTIMATION OF RESPONSE TIME

In order to estimate the response time of a system, a suitable model must be formulated on which to base the calculations. In practice, this model is very complex because of the nature of the factors that affect it, such as the erratic behaviour of users and the variable overheads of process changing. However, a simple model can be formulated that gives a reasonable approximation to system behaviour, even though it cannot reveal the likely variation in behaviour that a detailed statistical analysis would give.

A simple model can be formed by balancing the amount of 'service' that the system can supply in a given time with the amount being demanded by the users. Clearly, supply must be greater than or equal to demand. (In practice it would never be equal because of the system overheads associated with scheduling.) Consider a situation where a user is performing, say, an edit command that requires C units of processor time. The user types a command every T seconds and then has to wait a time R before he receives a response back at the terminal. The user therefore requires C units of time every $T + R$

seconds. If there are N users performing similar operations on the machine, they will each be performing a command every T + R seconds, and so

$$N * C \leqslant T + R$$

Thus, as would be expected, increasing the number of users N also results in an increase in the response time R (assuming approximately constant times for typing and for processing).

For example, if there are twenty users of the machine each performing similar operations (say, editing) that require 0.5 seconds of CPU time, and the users spend 5 seconds of each interaction in thinking and typing, an average response time is given by

$$20 * 0.5 \simeq 5 + R$$

Therefore

response time R = 5 seconds

This simple model can be extended to cater for situations when users are not performing similar operations. For example, for students working in a typical teaching laboratory, nineteen short interactions might be needed to edit a file for every long interaction required to compile it. If compiling takes 5 seconds, then every 20 interactions consume

19 * 0.5 seconds CPU time editing
+ 1 * 5 seconds CPU time compiling.

If the processes are not subject to time slicing, then the time for an interaction is still T + R seconds. During the course of twenty interactions, elapsed time can be equated with CPU time allocated, to arrive at the formula

$$20 * (5 + R) = (19 * 0.5 + 1 * 5) * N$$

which with twenty users gives a response time R of 9.5 seconds. Thus, as would have been expected, injecting longer interactions into the workload results in an increase in the response time.

The behaviour of the system is quite different if the processes are subject to time slicing. The time to perform a simple interaction will still be T + R, where R is now the time that the process is waiting to be allocated a time slice and the time required to perform the necessary operation, for example, an edit command. For the longer interactions, the response time is T + n * R where n is the number of time slices required to complete the interaction. In the example just considered, for a time slice of 0.5 second, the edit commands are performed in one time slice and the compilations in ten time slices (that is, n = 10). Thus, again equating elapsed and CPU time during the course of twenty interactions gives elapsed time = 19 * (5 + R) + 1 * (5 + 10R) seconds

during which time it is still necessary to allocate a CPU time of

19 * 0.5 + 1 * 5 seconds per process

Consider again a situation where there are twenty users of the machine. Then

19 * (5 + R) + 1 * (5 + 10R) = (19 * 0.5 + 1 * 5) * 20

or

R = 6.5 seconds

Thus, the time for an interaction when editing might be 6.5 seconds and for compiling, which requires ten time slices, the response might be 65 seconds. It can be seen from this that the effect of time slicing is to reduce the response time for short interactions at the expense of an increased response time for interactions that require several time slices.

6.5 PROBLEMS

1. Describe in detail the objectives and operation of the software concerned with program scheduling within a simple time sharing system.

2. Distinguish between preemptive and non-preemptive scheduling.

3. Why is preemption essential for the success of a multiprogrammed computer system?

4. Consider a time-sharing system in which all users are typing simple editing commands requiring 100 ms of computing.
   (a) If it takes 5 seconds to type a command, how many users would you expect the system to support simultaneously, assuming approximately an instantaneous response on average? The time for a complete interaction = Time to type 1 line + Response time CPU.
   (b) What would the average response time be if 100 users were online?
   (c) Generalise the result of (b) and plot response time against number of users. How many users could be supported with a response time of 2 seconds?
   (d) Is it necessary to use time slicing for the system in (a)?
   (e) If one command in every twenty is a compilation requiring 4 seconds computing, how many users could be supported?
   (f) Assuming a run-to-completion, first-come-first-served scheduling policy, what is the average response time with 100

users? Generalise this result for N users and find the value of N that gives an average response of 2 seconds.

(g) If time slicing is used for the system as in (f) with a time slice of 100 ms, with 100 users, what is the expected response for:

    (a) edit commands

    (b) compilations?

Generalise this result for N users, and compare with the answer to (f).

(h) With the system of (g), what is the maximum number of users that can be serviced if the editing response must be 2 seconds or less? What is the corresponding compilation response time?

7 Scheduling – Algorithms

The previous chapter introduced the basic concepts associated with processor scheduling. A more theoretical view of processor scheduling will be given and algorithms that can be used in this area will be examined.

The approach to be adopted in scheduling depends on the workload of the system and, in particular, on whether the system is (a) deterministic or (b) non-deterministic. The first might include real-time control systems where the frequency at which interactions are required and the processor time required for each is known in advance. The second is the more common and includes general-purpose time-sharing systems where the user behaviour is more varied. In this case it is necessary to resort to optimising the expected performance using suitable probability distributions for arrival and execution times.

7.1 OBJECTIVES OF SCHEDULING

In chapter 6 four aspects of system behaviour were identified that might be optimised:

(1) response/turnaround time
(2) meeting user specified deadlines
(3) CPU utilisation
(4) utilisation of other system resources

The choice of an algorithm to optimise one of these aspects is dependent also on whether the behaviour of the system is deterministic, whether tasks that might be dependent on each other are being scheduled and even whether multiple processors are available.

7.1.1 Response/turnaround time

In trying to optimise response/turnaround times, it is important to remember that these times can be optimised for certain tasks only at the expense of others. A common aim is to minimise the average response/turnaround time; this tends to favour short jobs at the expense of longer ones. It is equivalent to minimising

$$\sum_{i=1}^{No.\ of\ tasks} f_i$$

where f_i is the finishing time for task T_i.

7.1.2 Meeting user-specified deadlines

Often it is necessary to take account of user-specified job priorities in the scheduling. In the deterministic case this reduces to the problem of minimising the average weighted response time

$$\sum_{i=1}^{No.\ of\ tasks} W_i * f_i$$

where W_i is a weighting factor that reflects the job priority.

Deadline scheduling is concerned with trying to complete each job before a certain specified time. An attempt can be made to minimise either maximum job lateness, that is

$$\mathrm{Max}_i (f_i - D_i)$$

where D_i is the deadline for job i, or the average job lateness, that is

$$\sum_{i=1}^{No.\ of\ tasks} \mathrm{Max}(f_i - D_i,\ 0)$$

The first case corresponds to minimising the worst effect on any one user by the scheduling decision, while the second corresponds to minimising the collective effect.

7.1.3 CPU utilisation

CPU utilisation, which is defined as the percentage of time for which the system is busy performing user tasks, will be affected by:

(1) Availability of work to do. Naturally, if there are no jobs waiting or interactions pending, there is no point in trying to optimise performance. The algorithms must therefore consider only time during which work is available.

(2) The job characteristics — that is whether the job can use the CPU continually or whether it halts frequently (for example, for input/output transfers). This is difficult to appraise and so it is usually assumed that the tasks to be scheduled fully utilise the processor. This is certainly realistic for jobs in a spooling system, where the only halts are for transfers to and from the backing store and are quite short.

(3) In a multiprocessor system, constraints may be placed on job sequencing because tasks are interrelated. In general, minimising the total run time for a set of jobs is equivalent to maximising CPU utilisation.

7.1.4 Utilisation of other resources

This is clearly dependent on the characteristics of the other resources.

7.2 DETERMINISTIC SCHEDULING FOR INDEPENDENT TASKS ON A SINGLE PROCESSOR

In a deterministic situation, certain features are known about all the tasks to be scheduled, notably: (a) execution time T_i, (b) weighting factor W_i, (c) deadline D_i. From this information, algorithms can be devised for some of the scheduling policies described.

(1) Minimising mean response time $(\Sigma\ f_i)$.
Tasks are sequenced in the order of non-decreasing execution time T_i, so that short jobs are favoured in preference to longer jobs.

(2) Minimising mean weighted response time $(\Sigma\ W_i * f_i)$.
Tasks are sequenced in the order of non-decreasing T_i/W_i, so that the weighting factor W_i takes account of user-specified priority.

(3) Minimising maximum lateness $(Max(f_i - D_i))$.
Tasks are sequenced in the order of non-decreasing D_i and, if two tasks have equal deadlines, then they are sequenced in the order of non-decreasing T_i.

(4) Minimising average lateness $(\Sigma\ Max(f_i - D_i,\ 0))$.

Although this can be computed, no simple algorithm exists to achieve this.

The behaviour of these algorithms can be demonstrated by considering the scheduling of five tasks whose execution times, weighting factors and deadlines are given below:

i	1	2	3	4	5
Ti	5	6	4	2	3
Wi	1	4	2	3	1
Di	5	10	15	5	3

It is found that the three different scheduling policies yield the following sequences:

    (1) Minimum mean response time: T4, T5, T3, T1, T2
    (2) Minimum weighted response time: T4, T2, T3, T5, T1
    (3) Minimum maximum lateness: T5, T4, T1, T2, T3

These results are immediately available from a single scan of the source data.

This type of scheduling is possible only if the characteristics of the jobs is known in advance. For non-deterministic scheduling, an examination of the behaviour of the algorithms relies on knowledge of simple queuing theory.

7.3 SIMPLE QUEUING SYSTEM

The model can be based on that shown in figure 7.1, where tasks join a queue before being allocated processor time.

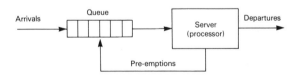

Figure 7.1 Simple queuing system

Certain properties of this system can be identified, namely: (a) arrival distribution, (b) service distribution, (c) queue length, (d) waiting time, (e) Little's result, (f) utilisation factor.

7.3.1 Arrival distribution

This determines the rate at which tasks come into the system. It is normally assumed to be exponential (partly for convenience, partly because this is a reasonable approximation to actual system behaviour). The exponential distribution is expressed as:

$$P(t) = \text{probability that no arrivals occur in time } t = e^{-\lambda t}$$

where λ is called the *arrival rate* and $1/\lambda$ is the mean *interarrival time*. The expected number of arrivals in time t is λt.

The exponential distribution exhibits what is known as the 'memoryless property'; that is, the probability of an arrival is not affected by the length of the waiting time. Arrivals with this distribution for arrival times constitute what are known as *Poisson* arrival processes.

7.3.2 Service distribution

This determines the service times of jobs entering the system. This is also normally assumed to be exponential:

$$F(t) = \text{probability that the service time is} \leqslant t = (1 - e^{-\mu t})$$

where μ is called the *service rate* and $1/\mu$ is the mean *service time*.

Again this exhibits the memoryless property; that is, the probability of a job finishing is not affected by how long it has already been running.

7.3.3 Queue length L

This is the number of jobs waiting in the system.

7.3.4 Waiting time W

This is the time a job has spent waiting.

7.3.5 Little's result

It can be seen that $L = \lambda W$ since in the steady state, when a job is in the queue for time W the number of arrivals (λW) exactly balances the number of jobs that leave the queue in this time (this equals the number of jobs in the queue before the job considered, that is, L).

7.3.6 Utilisation factor

This is a measure of how 'busy' the system is, and can be expressed as the mean number of arrivals during the service time of a single job. For exponential arrival and service distributions

$$\rho = \lambda/\mu$$

More generally

$$\rho = \int_0^\infty \lambda t \ dF(t)$$

7.4 SINGLE-PROCESSOR NON-DETERMINISTIC SCHEDULING

Now consider the more realistic cases in which arrival and execution times for jobs are not necessarily known in advance. Initially only scheduling algorithms appropriate to batch computing systems will be considered; three such algorithms will be examined in detail, namely:

(1) FCFS = First Come First Served
(2) SPT = Shortest Processing Time first (non preemptive)
(3) SRPT = Shortest Remaining Processing Time first (preemptive)

7.4.1 First-Come-First-Served Scheduling (FCFS)

Consider a new job joining the queue. Its wait time, W_{FCFS}, is given by

W_{FCFS} = (i) service time of the job in execution on arrival

+ (ii) service times of jobs in the queue before it

The expected value for (ii) is given by (queue length * mean service time), and by Little's Result, queue length = λW_{FCFS}. Thus, denoting (i) by Wo

$$W_{FCFS} = Wo + \lambda W_{FCFS} * 1/\mu = Wo + \rho W_{FCFS} = \frac{Wo}{(1 - \rho)}$$

Wo is derived as follows. If a job of service time t were being executed on arrival, its expected remaining service time would be $t/2$. The probability of an arrival during execution of such a job is

$$t \ dF(t)$$

so the expected remaining service time is given by

$$W_0 = \int_0^\infty (t/2)\lambda t \, dF(t) = \lambda/2 \int_0^\infty t^2 \, dF(t)$$

For an exponential service distribution

$$W_0 = \lambda/\mu^2 = \rho/\mu$$

This gives

$$W_{FCFS} = \rho/(1 - \rho) * 1/\mu$$

(It is convenient to express wait time as a multiple of the mean service time $1/\mu$).

7.4.2 Non-preemptive Shortest Processing Time Scheduling (SPT)

Assuming that once a job arrives its execution time is known, an attempt can be made to minimise the mean response time by selecting the shortest task in the queue for execution. Obviously now the waiting time will depend on the execution time of the job, so W_{SPT} is defined as the wait time for a job of service time t under SPT scheduling, as follows:

$W_{SPT}(t)$ = (i) service time of job in execution on arrival
    + (ii) service time of jobs ($\le$ t) in queue on arrival
    + (iii) service time of jobs ($<$ t) that arrive after this one
        but overtake it in the queue

Since in (ii) and (iii) only those jobs with service times $\le$ t are of interest, it is convenient to define λ_t, μ_t, ρ_t and L_t as the arrival rate, service rate, utilisation factor and queue length respectively, if only these jobs are considered. Then (iii) is given by

$$L_t + \frac{1}{\mu_t} = \frac{1}{\mu_t} * W_{SPT}(t) = \rho_t W_{SPT}(t)$$

Thus

$$W_{SPT}(t) = \frac{(i) + (ii)}{(1 - \rho_t)}$$

Denoting (i) + (ii) by U_t, it can be seen that this represents the steady-state amount of work in the system if jobs in the queue with execution times $>$ t are ignored. Since the arrival and service rates are fixed, U_t does not depend on the scheduling algorithm used and so it will be the same for all scheduling algorithms. Hence U_t can be calculated using an 'easy' scheduling algorithm such as FCFS. Ignoring all jobs in the queue with execution times $>$ t, it is clear that

$$U_t = W_0 + \rho_t U_t = \frac{W_0}{(1 - \rho_t)}$$

using the same argument as for FCFS above, and hence

$$W_{SPT}(t) \simeq \frac{Wo}{(1 - \rho_t)^2}$$

[ρ_t is given by $\int_o^t \lambda x \; dF(x)$, as compared with $\int_o^\infty \lambda x \; dF(x)$ for ρ]

Thus, for very short jobs

$$(\rho_t = 0), \; W_{SPT}(t) = Wo$$

for very long jobs

$$(\rho_t = \rho), \; W_{SPT}(t) = Wo/(1 - \rho)^2$$

and for 'average' jobs

$$(t = 1/\mu, \; \lambda_t = 1/4\rho), \; W_{SPT}(t) = Wo/(1 - 1/r\rho)^2$$

This illustrates that SPT scheduling gives an improvement in waiting time for short jobs as compared with FCFS, at the expense of longer jobs whose wait times become large as system loading increases (ρ tends to 1).

7.4.3 Shortest Remaining Processing Time Scheduling (SRPT)

The preemptive version of SPT scheduling always runs the job with the shortest remaining processing time. Thus if a new arrival has an execution time shorter than that remaining for the current job, the current job will be preempted and the new one run. This removes the dependence of the waiting time on the quantity Wo. In fact, as a first approximation:

$$W_{SRPT}(t) = \frac{To}{(1 - \rho_t)^2}$$

where To is a smaller quantity than Wo, as it is the expected service time of the job in execution if this is < t, and zero otherwise

[$To = \lambda/2 \int_o^t x^2 \; dF(x)$ as compared with $Wo = \lambda/2 \int_o^\infty x^2 \; dF(x)$].

For an exponential service time and for 'average' jobs ($t = 1/\mu$), To = 0.16W, and so for 'average' jobs SRPT scheduling produces an improvement in response by a factor of approximately six. For $t = 0$, To = 0; for $t = \infty$, To = W.

The above derivation ignores the fact that a job may continue to be overtaken even when it has started execution (the only arrivals considered are those occurring while the job is waiting). This will not make much difference for short jobs but will considerably extend the waiting times experienced by longer ones.

SRPT scheduling minimises mean waiting times in the system for any arrival and service distributions; even when all arrival and service times are known in advance, better mean service times cannot be achieved by other algorithms (this is a consequence of the use of preemption). Note that by Little's Result, the mean queue length and hence also the total storage space required is also minimised.

7.4.4 Comparison of response times

Figure 7.2 shows how wait times vary with system utilisation for jobs with $t = 1/\mu$ under the three algorithms discussed. The wait times are standardised (W/μ) so that a wait time equal to the mean service time is shown as 1.

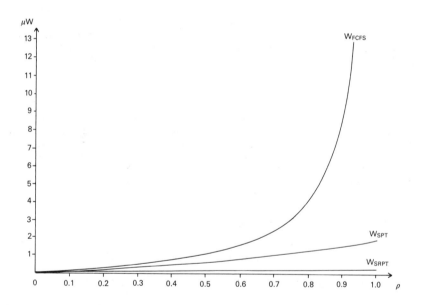

Figure 7.2 Effect of loading on response times

Note that both SPT and SRPT require that a job's execution time be known when it arrives. Often this is not the case and so some scheduling algorithms try to favour short jobs without explicit knowledge of execution times.

7.5 SINGLE-PROCESSOR TIME-SHARING SYSTEMS

In a time-sharing system the scheduling is primarily concerned with individual interactions of a job rather than complete jobs, although the general principle remains the same. The service time for an interaction is not normally known and so time slicing techniques are used to favour short ones. In chapter 6 this was illustrated with a simple model, and now expressions will be derived for the expected response times of the time-sharing system (a) when time slicing is not used, and (b) when using a simple time slicing algorithm, such as Round Robin.

7.5.1 Derivation of response in a time-sharing system with no time slicing

Consider a time-sharing system with N terminals, each capable of inputting commands at an average rate of λ, with average service times of $1/\mu$. Computation of the response times under these conditions is required. For the present, it will be assumed that tasks are input at a consistent rate of λ with a constant service time $1/\mu$, so that time slicing is unnecessary.

To illustrate the effect on response time, consider the following:
$$N = 50 \text{ terminals}$$
$$\lambda = 1 \text{ job every 10 seconds}$$
$$1/\mu = 1 \text{ second's computing.}$$

Here the users are trying to put more jobs into the system than it can service. The result, inevitably, is that a queue for service develops and so the response time increases. The effect of an increase in response time is a decrease in the effective input (arrival) rate for each user. In practice it is known that the rates at which work arrives in and leaves the system must be equal in a steady state:

Each terminal inputs a command every $(R + 1/\lambda)$ seconds

So from one terminal, there is a demand for $1/\mu$ seconds computing every $(R + 1/\lambda)$ seconds. From N terminals, the arrival rate and hence demand on CPU time is

N/μ seconds computing every $(R + 1/\lambda)$ seconds

On average, work cannot be input faster than it can be dealt with, so

$$N/\mu \leqslant (R + 1/\lambda)$$

This gives a response time of

$$R \geqslant (N/\mu - 1/\lambda) \text{ seconds}$$

which gives a response time curve of the form shown in figure 7.3.

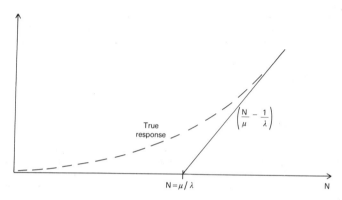

Figure 7.3 Response curve in a time-sharing system

In the region of interest (around saturation when $N = \mu/\lambda$), the actual curve will look something like the dotted line shown. Thus a more accurate model is needed to deal with these cases; heavily overloaded systems quite accurately follow the $(N/\mu - 1/\lambda)$ rule.

The inaccuracy in the above analysis is due to the '$\geqslant$' sign in the formula for R. This arises if the system is underloaded because work performed is actually *less than* the total available capacity. Work actually done can be zero if the system is idle, so the processing capacity available in time t is $(1 - \rho_o)$ where ρ_o is the probability that *all* terminals are idle. So, the formula becomes

$$R = \frac{N}{\mu(1 - \rho_o)} - \frac{1}{\lambda}$$

Note that R is a measure of the total amount of work in the system at the time a job arrives.

The value of ρ_o can be calculated quite easily if it is assumed that the rest of the system is idle. For a given terminal

$$\text{the proportion of time spent idling} = \frac{1/\lambda}{1/\lambda + 1/\mu} = \frac{\mu}{\mu + \lambda}$$

So the probability that all terminals are idle is

$$\rho_0 = \frac{\mu}{\mu + \lambda} \cdot N$$

Note that $\rho_0 \to 0$ for a very heavily loaded system, so that under heavy overload conditions the $(N/\mu - 1/\lambda)$ expression is in fact accurate.

7.5.2 Derivation of response in a time-sharing system using a Round Robin algorithm for time slicing

Time slicing in its simplest form of a Round Robin scheduling algorithm is a technique for giving a fast response to short interactions. Each job in turn is allocated an amount Q of time, its time slice. If it does not complete (that is, interact with its terminal) within this time, it is moved to the end of the queue of jobs requiring time, thus waiting while all other jobs receive a time slice before executing again. Obviously this means that if R′ is the response time for an interaction that requires a service time of Q, then a job requiring a service time of t > Q will experience a response time

$$R(t) = \frac{t}{Q} R'$$

The response time R′ for a trivial request (that is, one with t < Q) will now be determined. This is equal to the total time allotted to all the requests that were in the queue when it arrived (new arrivals + preemptions). In the worst case this would be $(N-1)Q$, but in practice

(a) not all the requests will use their full time slice

(b) not all the other $(N - 1)$ processes need be in the queue

Considering (a), the average time actually used, q $(< Q)$, should replace Q.
[This can be computed as the mean of the truncated distribution

$$F(t) = (1 - e^{-\mu t}) \qquad t \leqslant Q$$
$$= 1 \qquad t > Q$$

which has a mean value q given by

$$q = \frac{1}{\mu} \cdot (1 - e^{-\mu Q})]$$

Now, recall that the response time calculated in 7.5.1 gives the total amount of work in the system at the time a job arrives and observe that this is independent of the scheduling algorithm. On average, this represents a queue length of $R/(1/\mu) = R\mu$ jobs, and so the response time for trivial requests will be given by Rq. This gives

$$R' = \left(\frac{N}{1 - \rho_o} - \frac{\mu}{\lambda} \right) q$$

as the mean response to trivial requests, from which the response to other requests can be calculated. Notice that, using straightforward Round Robin scheduling, the response time with a given N is a constant multiple of service time. (In the above calculation the memoryless property of the exponential service distribution is implicitly used in calculating the queue length, as it was assumed that the mean service times of all jobs in the queue were equal -- with an exponential distribution, preempted jobs returned to the queue will have the same expected service time as new arrivals.)

7.5.3 The overheads of preemption

In the above, it has been assumed that processing requirements are dominant in determining response times and that there are no overheads incurred as a result of preemptions. In practice, in a time-sharing system a job will have to be swapped to store at the start of its time slice, and swapped out again at the end.

The effect of swapping on responses depends on exactly how the swapping is organised. If the time to swap a job in and out is s, and there is insufficient store space to overlap swapping of one job with execution of another, then the effective service time for a time slice becomes (q + s) instead of q, and the response times increases to

$$\left(\frac{N}{1 - \rho_o} - \frac{N}{\lambda} \right) (q + s).$$

If swapping and execution can be fully overlapped, then response time is not affected by swapping. This, however, requires that on average q > s, that is, jobs execute on average for longer than their swap times. If this is not so, then some processor time will be wasted waiting for swapping. Then

effective service time = Max(q, s)

and

$$\text{response time} = \left(\frac{N}{1 - \rho_o} - \frac{\mu}{\lambda} \right) * \text{Max}(q, s)$$

Obviously, in a real system, even if the average value of q exceeds the swap time, there will be some interactions for which it is very much less, and so in general there will be some free processor time. Provided that there is sufficient room in store, this free time can be used by keeping in core one or more jobs that used up their time slices without completing an interaction. These may then be run in any 'free time' that is available.

One useful idea is to try and identify 'non-interactive' jobs − say those that do not complete an interaction in less than some threshold time - and remove them from the time slicing cycle. It can then be arranged to keep one such job in memory at all times, possibly scheduling on an FCFS basis, to be run when the interactive jobs cannot use the processor. This has two main advantages. Firstly, the number of jobs in the time slicing queue is reduced and hence the interactive response is improved. Secondly, the average response time for the longer tasks is improved by not time slicing them with other long tasks. (Consider for example, ten 10-second jobs, time sliced in 100 ms slots. All jobs get a 100-second response in this case. If they are run on an FCFS basis, the first gets a 10-second response, the second 20 seconds and so on, giving an average response of 55 seconds.)

7.6 REFERENCES

A. O. Allen (1980). 'Queueing Models of Computer Systems', *Computer*, Vol. 13, pp. 13-24.

E. G. Coffman and P. J. Denning (1973). *Operating System Theory*, Prentice-Hall, Englewood Cliffs, N. J..

E. G. Coffman (ed.) (1976). *Computer and Job/Shop Scheduling Theory*, Wiley, New York.

P. Brinch Hansen (1973). *Operating System Principles*, Prentice-Hall, Englewood Cliffs, N. J..

7.7 PROBLEMS

1. Describe the objectives of scheduling algorithms.

2. Discuss the effects on response time of different scheduling algorithms used for a single processor.

3. Assuming that the arrival of processes satisfies the exponential distribution, and that jobs arrive at a computer at a rate of 30 per hour, then at any time calculate how long one would expect to wait for the next job to arrive, and how long it is before N jobs have been received.

4. The table below gives values for five jobs to be scheduled for single processor scheduling for independent tasks:

Job	1	2	3	4	5
Execution time	5	6	4	2	3
Weighting factor	1	4	2	3	1
Deadline	5	10	15	5	3

(a) What are the sequences for these tasks to achieve the following:
  (i)   minimum mean response time
  (ii) minimum weighted response time
  (iii) minimum maximum lateness?

(b) Repeat (a), but with the following constraints:
  (i) jobs 1 and 3 must be completed before job 2 starts
  (ii) jobs 3 and 4 must be completed before job 5 starts.

5. In a certain time-sharing system, each user spends an average of 20 seconds thinking and typing between interactions. The majority of interactions require 50 ms of CPU time, but one in twenty requires 2 seconds. In addition each interaction involves swap-in and swap-out times of 100 ms each.

Describe the scheduling and swapping policies to be adopted in this system to achieve the fastest possible response time for the maximum number of users.

Indicate how much store your system would require (in terms of the typical job size). Derive an expression for the response time R for short interactions, in terms of the number of users N. What are the assumptions and inaccuracies of this?

6. Give a single-processor algorithm that minimises the weighted sum of finishing times for a set of tasks whose execution times are known in advance. In a certain single-processor time-sharing system, the mean time a user spends thinking and typing between interactions is T seconds, and the mean CPU time used per interaction is t seconds. Assuming Round Robin scheduling with a time slice of q seconds, derive an expression for the response time R for trivial interactions as a function of T, t, q and the number of logged-in users, N. Give an approximate formula that agrees with this result for a system under heavy load, and sketch the accurate and approximate curves for R against N for the values T = 10 seconds, t = 0.25 seconds, and q = 0.1 seconds.

8 Memory Management – Basic Principles

The allocation of storage to the processes in a time-sharing system poses one of the most major problems to the designer of operating systems. If the system is supporting a large number of user processes, say N, in general it is impractical to keep all of them in memory, as on average only 1/N of the store will be in use at any given instant. Apart from the process that is currently running, some processes will be waiting for a time slice and some (usually the overwhelming majority) will be waiting for a response from the user. This latter category is the most problematic, as the typical response that can be expected from the user might be of the order of a few seconds (but might even be hours). Clearly, the system should not allow such a valuable commodity as its main storage to be underutilised to such an extent.

In most time-sharing systems, this problem is overcome by a technique known as swapping:

> Inactive processes are kept on the backing store in the form of a *core image*. Whenever the user interacts and is expecting a response, the process is allocated a time slice and the core image is loaded into memory before the process is re-started. On completion of the time slice, or when the process is waiting for the user to respond again, the core image may be transferred back to the backing store.

The backing store, often referred to as the secondary storage, may in practice consist of a hierarchy of storage devices, varying in capacity and speed from comparatively small, fast fixed head discs, to slow but larger exchangeable discs or similar mass storage devices. Similarly, the main memory, or primary storage, may be augmented by high speed cache stores. In a typical system, the memory management software might have to organise the swapping of programs between any of these levels in the storage hierarchy, although the management of the cache stores is in general a function of the hardware.

Irrespective of the number of levels in the storage hierarchy, the principles involved in swapping are basically the same as if only a single backing store and main memory existed. This two level structure will therefore be assumed when considering store management techniques.

Swapping naturally incurs an overhead and so great care is needed as to when to transfer a program into or out of store. For example, simple input/output operations to the terminal may be buffered by the operating system, thus avoiding having to keep the process in memory while the user is typing.

8.1 SWAPPING STRATEGIES

There are several variations in technique for swapping programs. These may vary in (a) the total amount of store required and (b) the time lost as a result of swapping. In particular, this latter factor may have a constraining effect on the number of terminals that can be serviced with a reasonable response time. To illustrate this, the behaviour of a number of different swapping strategies will be considered.

8.1.1 Simple swapping system

The simplest case would be a system where the main memory is large enough for just the operating system and a single user process, and all processes have to be swapped into the single space when they are allocated a time slice. This situation is illustrated in figure 8.1.

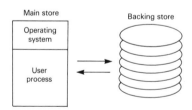

Figure 8.1 Simple swapping system

The criteria used for assessing the swapping strategy, namely the store and speed requirements, show:

    store size = 1 process + operating system

time for each interaction = swap in time + CPU time + swap out time
                           = 2 * swap time + CPU time

The CPU time will vary according to what the process is doing, up to a maximum value given by the time slice period.

Assessing the efficiency of this system as

$$\frac{\text{useful time}}{\text{total time}} * 100 \text{ per cent}$$

then

$$\text{CPU utilisation} = \frac{\text{CPU time}}{2 * \text{swap time} + \text{CPU time}} * 100 \text{ per cent}$$

The performance of this system is quite clearly dependent on the behaviour of the user process and the amount of CPU time it actually consumes whilst swapped into memory for its time slice. If the CPU time needed to process an interaction is quite short, the formulae show that there is a poor CPU utilisation but quite a rapid response for the user, with the swap time being the dominant factor. It is worth noting that this is one of the most major problems with time-sharing systems, where highly interactive jobs result in a low overall utilisation.

For interactions that require a large amount of CPU time, such as running a large compilation, the CPU utilisation is naturally much better. However, it is still dominated by the swap time, as the processes have to be time sliced in order to guarantee a reasonable response time.

The performance of this system is made more clear by considering in detail the behaviour of a typical exchangeable disc drive [DEC, 1980]. The time to swap a process in or out could be calculated as follows:

average head movement time	=	55 ms
minimum head movement time	=	15 ms
rotational speed	=	25 ms/revolution
average latency (1/2 revolution)	=	12.5 ms
capacity/track	=	10 K bytes

The time to transfer a (fairly small) process of 20 K bytes is therefore:

average head movement + 1/2 revolution latency + 1 revolution transfer
    (for first track)
+ minimum head movement + 1/2 revolution latency + 1 revolution transfer
    (for each subsequent track)
    = 55 + 12.5 + 25 + 15 + 12.5 + 25
    = 145 ms

A typical time slice period on such a system might be 1/10 second (100 ms), and so:

$$\text{total time for an interaction} = 2 * 145 + 100 \text{ ms}$$
$$= 390 \text{ ms}$$

If the system had to guarantee a response time of less than 2 seconds, then it could support only 5 users on the machine at once. This is quite low, and indeed, the overall efficiency of the CPU is equally poor:

$$\text{CPU utilisation} = \frac{100}{390} * 100 \text{ per cent}$$

$$\approx 26 \text{ per cent}$$

Even this estimation is somewhat optimistic as it assumes that each job will use its 100 ms slice of computing time. If the interaction takes less time than that, the utilisation will be even worse.

8.1.2 A more complex swapping system

The disadvantage with the simple swapping system is that the CPU is idle whilst a process is being transferred in and out of store, and even with CPU limited jobs and a comparatively large time slice period, the swap time is still the dominant factor. The natural development to alleviate this problem is to try to overlap some of the swapping with the computing in another user process. For this, the system has to be able to hold more than one process in store at a time, as illustrated in figure 8.2.

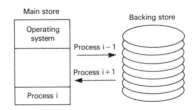

Figure 8.2 A more complex swapping system

With this scheme, process i executes while the previous process (process i-1) is swapped out and the next (process i+1) is swapped in.

This system relies on the process executing for a time sufficient to swap one process out and another one in, and indeed, the maximum value assigned for a time slice period might be aimed at achieving this balance. If so, theoretically it may be possible to achieve 100 per cent CPU utilisation, although this is rather dependent on the jobs being CPU limited and consuming all of the time allocated to them. If the amount of processing is quite small, as is probably more typical, the performance would be comparable to that of the simple system.

Considering the performance figures from the previous example:

$$\text{store size} = 2 \text{ processes} + \text{operating system}$$

$$\text{total time for an interaction} = \text{Max}(\text{CPU time}, 2 * \text{swap time})$$
$$= 290 \text{ ms}$$

This implies that the system could support up to seven users with a guaranteed response time under 2 seconds. This is an improvement on the performance of the simple system, as is the overall efficiency:

$$\text{CPU utilisation} = \frac{100}{290} * 100 \text{ per cent}$$

$$\simeq 34 \text{ per cent}$$

8.1.3 Further developments of the swapping system

The more complex swapping system still has the disadvantage that its performance is dependent on the single user process that is currently in memory. If this does not use its full time slice, as is very probable with highly interactive jobs, the performance of the system is dominated by the times taken to go to and from the backing store. An extension of this system is therefore to provide for a number of processes to be in memory waiting to run (the precise number is arbitrary, but still considerably less than the total number in the machine). The following strategy can then be adopted:

(1) If a process waits for input/output, then it is likely to be waiting for several seconds before the next line is typed in and so it can be swapped out immediately.

(2) If a process is preempted because its time slice has run out, it is preferable to retain it in store. There is a good possibility that the process will be scheduled and run again without needing to reject it from memory. In addition, if the later processes do not use their full slice of CPU time, it might be possible to switch to those left in store to utilise the spare capacity. There is also a reduction in the loading of the disc channel owing to the elimination of wasteful and redundant disc transfers.

The main disadvantage with this scheme is that it might lead to some quite complex scheduling and swapping strategies as a result of the close interaction between them. A variant of this algorithm is to keep one batch job in store (as a background process) which can always be run to use any spare CPU capacity whilst swapping the interactive processes.

8.2 MEMORY PROTECTION

The second main problem with memory management in a time-sharing system is one of protection. Where there are a number of processes in the machine, the operating system has to protect each from interference by the others, not forgetting, of course, that it also has to protect itself from interference by the user programs. A number of techniques exist for protecting the resources in the system from illegal access by user programs. The more advanced techniques for this will be considered in chapter 14. In this and in chapter 9, the main consideration will be techniques specifically concerned with protecting storage.

In practice, the problem of protecting the operating system from a user is basically the same as protecting one user program from another.

In the simple system shown in figure 8.3, the user process is placed in store at location 0 and the operating system at the top of store. When the user job is running, it should be able to access only locations O to N, whereas when the operating system is running, addresses up to the store size S should be permitted.

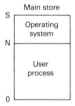

Figure 8.3 A simple memory organisation

The validity of addresses has to be checked by hardware as it must be performed on every store access and special hardware is the only efficient way of achieving this. If it is assumed that the operating system is trustworthy and so there is no need to check the addresses generated by it, the only check that must be applied is that no address greater than N is generated when in a user program. For the hardware to apply this check, it must know two items:

(1) Where the operating system starts, that is N (a special register could be used to hold this information).
(2) Whether the user program or the operating system is running at any instant in time.

The most common way of implementing this is by providing two modes of execution, a *user mode* and a *privileged mode*. In user mode only addresses 0 to N are valid, whereas in privileged mode, addresses 0 to S are permissible. The transition from user mode to privileged mode is performed either:

(1) When an interrupt occurs, at which time the value of the program counter is also set to an entry point in the operating system code.
(2) As the result of a special 'enter operating system' instruction.

Thus, privileged mode is set only when obeying operating system code.

Attempts to access non-existent locations or addresses in the operating system when in user mode result in a program fault interrupt. The interrupt entry sequence sets privileged mode and also sets the program counter to the start of an interrupt procedure in the operating system. Other program fault conditions have a similar effect, as do certain kinds of instructions, such as HALT, which are deemed to be illegal in user mode.

8.3 VIRTUAL ADDRESSING

The use of a limit register is an effective way of protecting the operating system from user programs, but it is insufficient in a general time-sharing system. If there are a number of user programs in store, it is impossible to start all of them at address 0 and so an additional mechanism within the hardware is necessary.

One option is to include a base register within the hardware so that both the starting and finishing addresses of the current program are known. The store accessing hardware could then check that addresses generated by the user programs lie within the specified region. This provides the necessary protection but has a number of significant drawbacks. If the operating system is time slicing the programs and swapping them in and out of memory, it is very inconvenient (and inefficient) if programs have to be loaded into precisely the same physical locations as they occupied on the previous time slice. Although programs may be compiled to be relocatable, it is not feasible to try to relocate a 'core image' at a different address at the start of each time slice.

The most satisfactory solution is to provide the relocation mechanism within the store accessing hardware itself. Each process therefore sees a *virtual store* that extends from address 0 up to some limit N. In practice, the program may reside in the real store starting at address B, as shown in figure 8.4.

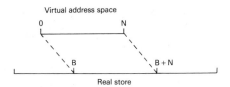

Virtual address space

Real store

Figure 8.4 Virtual store mapping

The translation between virtual and real addresses has to be performed for every store access in user mode, and this can be performed efficiently only if suitable hardware is provided between the CPU and the store. The most simple form of hardware for doing this translation is the base-limit register system shown in figure 8.5.

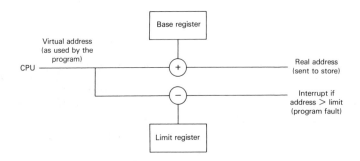

Figure 8.5 Base-limit register

Prior to entering a process, the coordinator sets the base register to the start of the memory allocated to it and the limit register to its size. This would be performed as part of the register reloading sequence executed normally when entering a process. When in user mode, all addresses are translated by adding the base register to the virtual address generated by the program. This produces a real address which is sent to the store.

A check is also made for addresses outside the permissible range of the program by comparing the virtual address with the limit register. If the virtual address is greater, then an interrupt is generated and the operating system entered to perform suitable remedial action (such as faulting the program or allocating more space).

The memory organisation of a typical system is illustrated in figure 8.6. Here, the time-sharing system is supporting a number of user processes, each with its own virtual address space starting at virtual address 0, but not constrained to any particular real address.

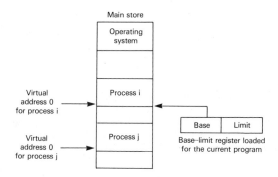

Figure 8.6. Memory management in a base-limit register system

The action of the store accessing hardware when the machine is in privileged mode varies between different computers. On some, an alternative set of address translation registers are provided for the system software, in effect providing the operating system with its own virtual address space. On other machines, the address translation mechanism is by-passed altogether so that the operating system uses real addresses.

8.4 REFERENCES

DEC (1980), 'RL01/02 Disks', *Peripherals Handbook*, Digital Equipment Corporation, Maynard, Massachusetts, U.S.A.

8.5 PROBLEMS

1. Explain the principles that lead to the use of base-limit registers.

2. Discuss the reasons to separate a user's virtual store from the real storage space.

3. Describe a technique used to map virtual addresses to real addresses.

9 Memory Management – Segmentation

The memory management system described in chapter 8 provides an adequate set of facilities for implementing a reasonable time-sharing system. Each user process has its own virtual store which is protected from interference by other processes by the use of the base-limit register. Additionally, this mechanism protects the operating system from illegal accesses by the user programs. Many early computers relied solely on this technique for implementing a suitable multi-access system, but there are still a number of major problems outstanding for the system designer, most notably: (a) fragmentation, (b) locality of programs and (c) sharing of data structures or code, such as compilers and editors. Each of these will now be considered.

9.1 FRAGMENTATION

The problem of fragmentation (or more specifically, external fragmentation), stems from the fact that processes are continuously being swapped in and out of store. The sizes of the processes vary with the effect that when a process is transferred out, a space is left in store which is of a variable size. Similarly, when transferring a process into store, a space must be found which is sufficient for it to fit into. The store is said to be fragmented if the free space is split into many small areas, and as a consequence there is a situation where

total free space > program size

yet there is no contiguous space large enough to hold the new program.

Fragmentation is largely dependent on the techniques used to maintain a pool of free space, and the allocation from this pool. For example, consider the following strategies:

(1) A single empty space could be maintained at the top of store by shuffling the programs down whenever a hole is created. This would

completely eliminate the problem of fragmentation but is very time-consuming as a lot of information may need to be transferred at the end of each time slice. This becomes increasingly ineffective if the size of the computer system (and correspondingly the main store) is large.

(2) The system might keep a list of free blocks (and their sizes), and the allocation algorithm might then allocate, say, the first hole it finds greater than the required size. If there isn't a space large enough, the technique might then resort to strategy (1). Alternatively, the allocation algorithm might be made more selective by allocating the smallest space which is large enough for the program. The idea behind this is to leave the biggest holes untouched. A consideration of these and other algorithms is presented in chapter 11.

(3) The programs already in store could be run until one of them finishes and leaves a large enough space. However, this might seriously affect the response time of the system through giving some programs an unduly long time slice.

Although fragmentation has only been considered in the context of allocating space in the main store, it should be remembered that exactly the same problems can occur when allocating space on the backing store.

9.2 PROGRAM LOCALITY

Program locality is largely concerned with the way programs use their virtual address space. Although the address space is uniform, that is all store locations have similar characteristics, the pattern of accesses to these store locations is far from being uniform. This gives rise to two main areas of inefficiency: (a) static sparseness and (b) dynamic sparseness.

(a) Static sparseness

The real store allocated must be equivalent to the range of virtual addresses used, even though the program might be using the space very sparsely.

Figure 9.1 illustrates a case in point, where a program has its code residing at one end of the virtual store and its data structures at the other. Unfortunately, real store has to be allocated to cover the space between, even though the program might never access it. There is also an extra time overhead to be suffered when swapping the program into store with having to transfer the redundant information.

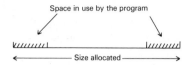

Figure 9.1 Sparse usage of the virtual address space

An immediate reaction might be that this was bad programming practice and that users who programmed in this way deserved poor efficiency from their computer system. However, consider how a compiler might arrange its data structures in store. This is illustrated in figure 9.2.

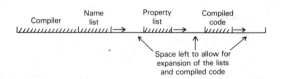

Figure 9.2 Possible memory organisation during compiling

The compiler must assign space for its data structures assuming it is compiling a very large program. Of course, with small programs most of the space assigned for the name list, property list, etc. will be unused. However, this is unavoidable unless an optimised compiler is provided specifically for small programs.

(b) Dynamic sparseness

The information accessed by a program during a time slice is often quite small. For example, the program might be running within a single procedure, operating on only one or two of its data structures. However, *all* of the program and data must be brought into store on *every* occasion. This situation is known as dynamic sparseness and is illustrated in figure 9.3.

9.3 SHARING OF CODE AND DATA

A number of cases have already been encountered where there is a logical need for programs to share store (for example, the document list providing the communication between , the input spooler and the job

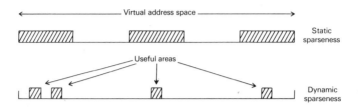

Figure 9.3 Comparison of static and dynamic sparseness

scheduler). There are also cases when it would be beneficial to be able to share code. For example, in a time-sharing system where there are a number of processes using the same compiler, the ability to share a single copy of the compiler's code between all programs has a significant and beneficial effect on both the total store occupancy and the swap times, as there is no need to swap a copy of the compiler in and out with each process.

In order to be able to share programs, they must be expressed as *pure code*, that is: (a) the program is not self-modifying in any way, (b) the data is kept separately from the program (and probably accessed via one or more registers which can be given different values in different processes). Quite clearly, a program that modifies itself cannot be shared, and neither can one whose data areas cannot be made different for each of the processes that use it.

Sharing in a controlled and protected way is extremely difficult to achieve in a single base-limit register machine. Consider, for example, the situation shown in figure 9.4.

In this case, code is being shared between two processes, each having its own data area. Although the base-limit register can be set for process 1 to restrict its address space to the code and its own data area, we are unable to do the same for process 2. This relaxation of the protection system might be permissible if the two processes are part of the operating system (and hence are tried and trusted). However, it is clearly unacceptable in the general case when user programs are needing to share code.

9.4 MULTIPLE BASE-LIMIT REGISTER MACHINES

The three problem areas of fragmentation, sparseness and sharing together have a serious effect on the overall efficiency of a time-sharing system. For this reason, most modern machines supporting large multi-access systems rely on alternative forms of memory management to help alleviate these difficulties.

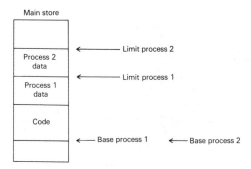

Figure 9.4 Sharing in a single base-limit register system.

In the case where information is shared between programs, there is an obvious way in which changes to the hardware can improve the situation. If there are two base-limit registers in the hardware, one can be used for translating the addresses for accesses to the code and the other for accesses to the data areas, as shown in figure 9.5. The hardware is aware of which register to use for address translation at any instant, as the control logic knows whether an instruction is being fetched or an operand being accessed.

This provides an effective means of sharing either the data area or the code area. It still has some deficiencies, however, as programs may want to share only part of their data or code area. For example, the programs might want to share a common table, but not share other data items such as those on the stack. The solution to this is to have several base-limit registers that can be used for the different data and code areas. For example, on a machine like the DEC PDP11/34 (and similar PDP11 machines [DEC, 1979]) there are eight base-limit registers for defining up to eight distinct areas for code or data.

When several base-limit registers are available to define the code and data areas, there has to be a means of deciding which of the registers is to be used for translating each virtual address. The distinction between instruction and operand accesses is no longer sufficient. Instead, the choice is usually achieved using a field within the virtual address itself. The virtual store is therefore divided into a number of areas or *segments*, each of which has its own base-limit register.

Segmentation should be regarded as a division of the virtual store into *logical* areas. Items with the same characteristics are therefore

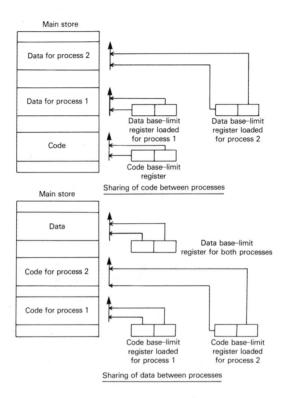

Figure 9.5 Use of two base–limit registers

grouped together in a segment. For example, there might be a segment for shareable code (a common library) and one for private code, one for the process stack, another for shared data structures, one for input and output buffers, etc.

9.5 ADDRESS TRANSLATION ON A MULTIPLE BASE–LIMIT REGISTER MACHINE

A machine designed with multiple base–limit registers could perform its address translation as shown in figure 9.6.

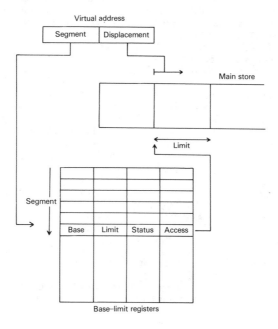

Figure 9.6 Multiple base-limit register system

A virtual address, as used by a program, is split into two parts. The segment field indexes into a table of base-limit registers. Once a register is selected in this way, the operation is similar to that in the single base-limit register system. The displacement part of the virtual address is added to the base to give the required real address. It is also checked against the limit of the register to ensure that the program does not try to access locations beyond the allocated size of the segment.

There are several important features about this system that influence the operating system design and its overall behaviour.

(1) The operating system maintains a *segment table* for each process that holds the base-limit values for each of the process segments. On process changing, the hardware base-limit registers are loaded from the segment table of the process being entered. On some machines this has to be performed by software, that is by the

coordinator as part of the register reloading sequence for the program. On other machines, loading of the registers is performed by the hardware when a special registers, known as the *Segment Table Base Register* is assigned the starting address of the segment table. On such machines, the layout of the operating system tables must conform with the format expected by the address translation hardware.

(2) As each segment has its own limit register, the amount of space allocated for mapping the virtual store can be restricted to a minimum. The system no longer needs to allocate real store to cover the unused areas in the virtual store and so the problem of static sparseness is resolved. In the extreme, some segments may even have a limit of zero, that is, be completely unallocated.

(3) The segment table entries might point to segments resident on the backing store. The operating system might then bring the segments into store only when they are accessed. This is known as *demand loading* and obeys the following sequence:

   (a) A program attempts to access a particular segment but the attempt fails as the status field in the base-limit register shows that the segment is not in memory.

   (b) A *virtual store interrupt* is generated and the operating system is entered with information about the required virtual address.

   (c) The operating system decodes the virtual address, loads the segment into memory and changes the segment table (and base-limit register) accordingly.

   (d) The program is restarted, re-executes the instruction that previously failed and proceeds.

   This partially solves the problem of dynamic sparseness as only segments currently being accessed need be loaded into memory. It is not a complete solution, however, as the whole segment has to be loaded even though accesses may be very localised.

(4) As it is unnecessary to load *all* of a program into memory at the same time, a much larger virtual store can be allowed than there is real store available. For example, many 32-bit machines allow a virtual address space of 2^{32} bytes. This is clearly much larger than the main store available on any machine. Naturally, if a program tries to access all of its virtual store at once, it cannot all fit into the main memory, and so segments may be swapped into and out of the store by the operating system while running the program.

(5) Division of a program into logical units allows much better protection to be provided for the individual segments. In particular,

It is possible to protect against faulty accesses, such as write accesses to the code segments. This is implemented with the aid of additional access permission bits in the base-limit registers. The permission field is checked on each store access to ensure that the required type of access is allowed. There might typically be at least three bits signifying:

read	reading of operands allowed
write	write to operands allowed
obey	instruction fetch accesses allowed

A fourth permission bit is often provided to distinguish segments in the virtual store that are accessible only to the operating system.

The use of these access permission bits again emphasises that segmentation is a logical division of the virtual store, where items with similar characteristics and access modes are grouped together. For a simple program, such as an editor, there might be segments for:

code	obey only (or obey and read)
input file	read only
output file	read and write
stack	read and write

The operating system might also keep a fifth permission bit in the segment table entries. This is not accessed by the hardware but indicates whether a user is allowed to change the access permission associated with the segment.

9.6 SHARED SEGMENTS

Division of the virtual store into segments opens up a convenient and logically clean way of sharing information between processes, as individual segments can be shared without reducing the protection that each process expects for the rest of its virtual store. The organisation of the operating system tables still presents a problem to the system designer, as there are at least three distinct ways in which the tables can be structured. These will be identified as: (a) all direct, (b) one direct, all others indirect, (c) all indirect.

The choice of technique for any particular system might depend to a large extent on the hardware support for reloading the base-limit registers, as well as on other performance constraints.

9.6.1 All direct

In this scheme, as shown in figure 9.7, the processes sharing the segment each have their own segment table entry with a copy of the base-limit values for the segment. Note that:

(1) The segment number does not need to be the same in each user's virtual store. For example, segment 1 in process A might be the same as segment 3 in process B.

(2) A complication arises if the segment has to be moved (for example, swapping it into and out of store) as all of the segment tables pointing at it must be altered accordingly. This leads to complicated list structures where the segment tables are linked together. In some respects, therefore, it is not a good technique, as it incurs significant run-time overheads in maintaining the system tables.

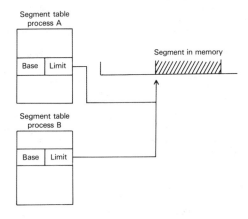

Figure 9.7 Shared segments, all direct

9.6.2 One direct, all others indirect

In this system, shown in figure 9.8, the principal user has a direct pointer (a base-limit value) from its segment table to the required segment in store. Other processes have to use indirect pointers from their segment tables into the segment table of the principal user, and thence indirectly access the relevant segment in store. In this case, note that:

(1) An indirect bit is required in the segment table entries to determine whether the entry is pointing directly at the segment or at another segment table entry. If the base-limit registers are loaded by

hardware, this additional status bit will need to be recognised by the address translation mechanism.

(2) This scheme is satisfactory if the owner of the segment is permanent, but situations may arise where the system needs to move the segment table for the owner (such as between time slices when the process is otherwise dormant), or where the owning process terminates or when it is necessary to delete the segment from the virtual store.

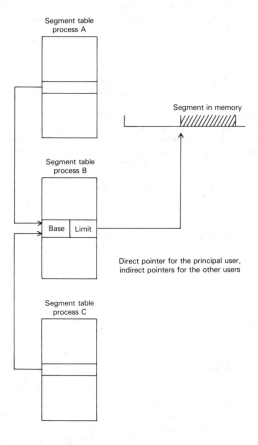

Figure 9.8 Shared segments, one direct, all others indirect

9.6.3 All indirect

The system involving only indirect pointers to shared segments is shown in figure 9.9. This seeks to improve on the deficiencies found in the previous system by maintaining a separate table for the shared values of the base-limit registers. This table is often called either the *global segment table* or the *system segment table*. Although it is possible to use this table only for segments which are shared, and otherwise to use direct pointers in the process segment tables, it is usually more convenient, and simple, if the system segment table holds details of *all* base-limit register addresses known to the system. Each process has its own *local segment table* and this provides a pointer into the system segment table from which the relevant base-limit information can be obtained. A segment is shared by having identical pointers. In this case:

(1) If the segment is moved, only one table, namely the system segment table, needs to be altered.

(2) The system segment table defines all the segments known to the operating system. The index into this table (the system segment number SSN) therefore provides a unique identification for the segment. This is often used elsewhere within the operating system when referring to the segment.

(3) The system segment table is *never* moved, so there is no difficulty with updating the pointers from the individual local segment tables.

(4) The local segment table entries hold the access permission that each user has to the segments. Therefore, users can have different access permissions to the same segment. For example, one user may have read and write access permission; a second (less-trusted user) may only be able to read the segment.

(5) The base-limit value is in the system segment table so that users sharing a segment share *all* of the segment. This again is in keeping with the notion of a segment being a single logical entity and, as such, each segment is indivisible.

9.7 COMMON SEGMENTS

A rather special case of sharing information concerns the provision of certain frequently used software, such as compilers, editors, mathematical libraries, etc. Ideally, if the machine is capable of providing for a large virtual address space, it would be convenient to preload all of these facilities directly into the user's virtual store. The facilities would then be readily available to the process without having to go through a sequence of opening libraries, etc. It would be possible, of course, to include entries for all of these frequently accessed

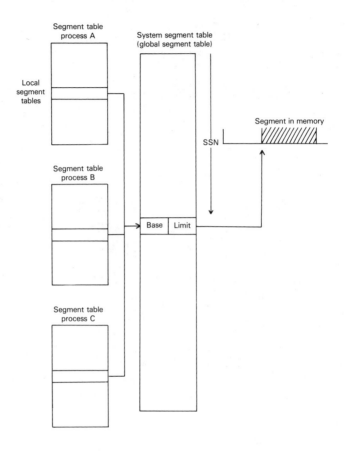

Figure 9.9 Shared segments, all indirect

segments in each process segment table, although this would be very wasteful as the same information would be duplicated for all processes.

A solution is to have a separate table of common segments. All virtual addresses above a certain segment number are translated with the information in the *common segment table*, rather than the entries in the local segment tables. Such a system is shown in figure 9.10.

This scheme might also have additional benefits if the loading of the

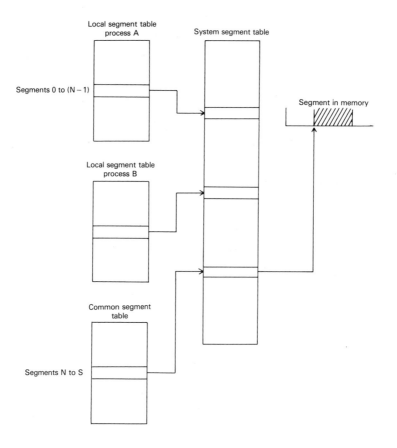

Figure 9.10 Segmentation with common segments

base–limit registers is performed by software, as only the first N registers have to be reloaded when changing processes.

This optimisation might also apply to systems where the hardware automatically loads the base–limit registers, as such machines will have *two* segment table base registers, one for the local segment table of the current process and one for the common segment table.

9.8 REFERENCES

DEC (1979), *PDP11 Processor Handbook,* Digital Equipment Corporation, Maynard, Massachusetts, U.S.A.

9.9 PROBLEMS

1. Why do some operating systems provide segmented virtual stores? Outline some ways in which they might be implemented.

2. Explain how fragmentation occurs and distinguish between dynamic and static sparseness.

3. Discuss the advantages and disadvantages of non-contiguous storage allocations.

4. Describe the mapping of virtual addresses to real addresses in the case of shared segments.

10 Memory Management – Paging Systems

In chapters 8 and 9 it was shown how the multiple base-limit system evolved in an effort to solve the problems inherent in the single base-limit register system. The problems of sharing and sparseness have largely been resolved, although in the case of dynamic sparseness the solution is not entirely satisfactory as whole segments have to be transferred in and out of memory in order to access just a single location. However, there are still problems with the segmented system, namely: (a) fragmentation and (b) a potential deadlock situation when a number of jobs are being multiprogrammed, since although all the processes have some of their segments in store, the number may not be enough to run (or at least to run efficiently).

10.1 PAGING

The problem of fragmentation arises because storage space is allocated in variable sized units. The solution, in simple terms, is to allocate store only in fixed sized units. This concept is known as *paging*, where the user's addressing space is split into a number of pages of equal size. Although this division is not immediately apparent to the user, the virtual address must be structured in order to allow mapping of the pages on to the real store. The address translation mechanism therefore assumes a format for the virtual address as shown in figure 10.1.

This division should not be confused with that seen with segmentation. Segmentation was defined to be a logical division of the virtual store, where the segments could be of a variable size and with different protection attributes. Thus, a segment might contain a complete text file or a compiler. Paging is a practical division of the virtual store, intended primarily to avoid the problems of fragmentation. The pages are of a fixed size, and are usually considerably smaller than the size normally required for segments.

Figure 10.1 Virtual address space

The main disadvantage with paging is that space may be wasted if only very small areas of store are required, as the smallest unit that can be allocated is a page. This problem is known as internal fragmentation, and its main effect is on the choice of the page size for a machine.

10.2 ADDRESS TRANSLATION IN A PAGED MACHINE

The mapping of virtual addresses on to the real store poses a number of problems not encountered with the segmented systems. The number of pages in each process virtual store is usually quite large. For example, page sizes typically vary between 1/2 Kbyte and 4 Kbytes, so that on a machine with a 32 bit virtual address, each process might have between one and eight million pages. Although it may be possible to apply certain restrictions on the user so that a much more limited virtual addressing space is used, the number of pages required by a process is still quite large.

The mapping of a large number of pages precludes the use of base registers such as those described in chapter 9 for segmented machines. To avoid the high cost of these registers, a logically equivalent technique would be to have a page table for each process resident in memory, as illustrated in figure 10.2. This is indexed by the page field of the virtual address to yield the corresponding real page number.

The main disadvantage with this technique, apart from the very large size of the page table, is that every location accessed would require an additional memory access in order to translate the virtual address. Clearly, suitable caching of the page table entries would be required to avoid a significant degradation in the overall system performance.

10.2.1 Address translation using page address registers

The very first paged machine was Atlas (Kilburn, 1962). This resolved the problem of translating addresses in an efficient way by having a register associated with each page of real memory. These registers, illustrated in figure 10.3, were known as page address registers (PARs).

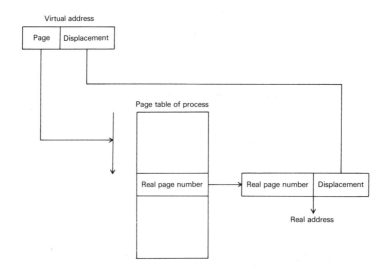

Figure10.2 Direct mapping of virtual address in a paged machine

The page address registers were associative registers holding the virtual address corresponding to each page of real memory. When making a store access, the page field of the virtual address was presented to all of the page address registers in parallel. If the required page was in memory, then one of the registers signalled equivalence with the virtual page number, and the address translation mechanism arranged to access the corresponding real page. Thus, accesses to the pages of a process could be performed very quickly without having to make redundant memory accesses.

If none of the page address registers signalled equivalence at the time of making a store access, then the required page was not available in memory and so a virtual store interrupt was generated. The operating system then had to examine the page table to discover the whereabouts of the required page.

In practice, the Atlas system did not maintain a page table for each process as described earlier. As this page table is never accessed by the address translation mechanism (as pages in store would already have been translated by the page address registers), a more compact representation was desirable. Thus, the operating system maintained a page table that held both a virtual page number and the corresponding real address of the page. This, of course, had to be searched sequentially by the operating system in order to find the location of the

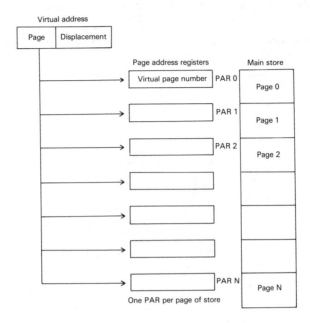

Figure 10.3 Address translation using page address registers

required page. Nevertheless, the trade off between search time and page table space was clearly advantageous, as the searching occurred only when there was liable to be a substantial delay in bringing the required page into memory.

10.2.2 Address translation using current page registers

The major disadvantage with machines that use page address registers is that the address translation mechanism is very closely linked with the actual memory organisation. Thus if the amount of memory on a machine is changed, there has to be a corresponding change in the number of page address registers. In addition to this being rather inflexible, the cost of the fast associative registers is prohibitive, particularly when very large memory sizes are considered. Nevertheless, mechanisms based on the page address register organisation still appear in modern computer designs (Edwards, 1980).

An alternative mechanism that is very widely used is based on associative registers known as current page registers. On machines using these, there is no longer a direct correspondence between current page registers and memory pages. Instead, the current page registers have an additional field which indicates the page of memory to which the virtual page number applies. This is illustrated in figure 10.4.

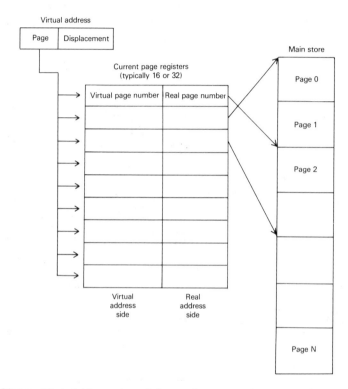

Figure 10.4 Address translation using current page registers

With this address translation scheme, the page field of the virtual address is sent to each of the current page registers in parallel. As with the page address registers, if the virtual address is mapped by the current page registers, one of the registers signals equivalence. The starting address of the corresponding block of memory is obtained from the real address side of the register and this is concatenated with the displacement field to yield the required real address.

If none of the registers signals equivalence, it does not necessarily mean with this scheme that the required page is not in memory, only that there is not a current page register pointing at the page. In this case, the address translation system has to access the page table in order to find the location of the required page. If the status information in the page table shows that the page is in main memory, then a current page register can be loaded to point to the required page. If the page is not in memory, a virtual store interrupt is generated and the operating system has to retrieve the page.

10.3 PAGED SEGMENTED MACHINES

One of the disadvantages with the paged systems described so far is the large page table that has to be maintained for each process. Although this was avoided in the Atlas implementation, that technique relied on providing a complete mapping of the real store using page address registers. Systems using current page registers for their address translation rely on the hardware being able to access the system tables for reloading the registers. This precludes the associative searching of page tables, as occurred with Atlas. Clearly, some way of structuring the system tables to provide a more compact organisation is desirable, while still retaining the ability to index into the data structures to obtain a particular page table entry.

A very effective solution is clearly illustrated on machines that combine the techniques of both paging and segmentation. The intention of these machines is to enjoy the benefits of a segmented virtual store, as with the multiple base-limit register machines, while using paging to eliminate the problems of external fragmentation (Daley, 1968; Buckle, 1978; Kilburn, 1968). The virtual addressing space on these machines is divided into fields as shown in figure 10.5.

Figure 10.5 Paged Segmented Addressing

In this case there are three fields in each address giving:

(a) segment
(b) page within a segment
(c) displacement within a page

The retrieval of the real address of a page is therefore achieved by successively indexing into a segment table and page table, as shown in figure 10.6.

The tables used for address translation can be regarded as forming a tree structure with the program list at the top level.

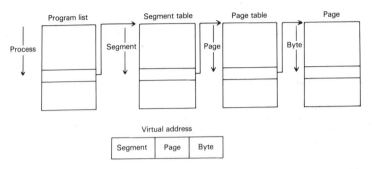

Figure 10.6 Address translation using segment and page tables

Program list   This has one entry per process and contains a pointer
                   to the segment table for each process.

Segment table   There is one segment table per process, which
                   describes the segments available to a process, and
                   the location of the page table for each of those
                   segments.

Page table   Each segment has a page table, which gives the
                   location of all of the pages within that segment.

Although this structure potentially occupies considerably more table
space than the simple linear page table described earlier, this system
relies on two important factors. Firstly, programs do not access all of
the segments available in the virtual store and so page tables will not
need to be allocated for undefined segments. Secondly, the page
tables can be swapped in and out of memory so that only those for
segments currently in use need be resident in memory.

10.4 STORE MANAGEMENT IN A PAGED SEGMENTED MACHINE

The remainder of this chapter examines the structure and operation of a
typical store management system. The algorithms and data structures
have been chosen purely as an illustration of how a simple system might
be organised. Many other techniques are possible, and some alternative
algorithms are presented in chapter 11.

The main data structures of the store management system are the
segment and page tables that map the virtual store on to the real store.
To a great extent, the format of these is defined by the address

translation hardware of the machine. It is therefore the responsibility of the system architect in specifying the address translation system to ensure that the virtual store has the desired characteristics. A fairly typical organisation is shown in figure 10.7. This is based on the paged segmented structure already outlined, with the additional refinement of allowing process and system segment tables to assist in the sharing of segments. The provision of common segments would also be possible, although it has been omitted in this example for the sake of simplicity.

10.4.1 Segment table base register

The root of the address translation system is the segment table base register. This contains the address of the segment table for the current process, and hence defines the virtual address space currently accessible. This register is reloaded on process changing, with the effect that an entirely new virtual store is brought into use. In addition to the address of the segment table, this register might also contain a limit field giving the size of the process segment table, and hence the maximum segment number accessible by the process.

10.4.2 Process segment table

Each process segment table has three fields which serve the following functions.

(1) Status

This indicates whether the segment has been defined by the user. As all segments have attributes, such as a size and access permission, it is necessary for users to tell the operating system whenever a segment is required and the attributes to be associated with it. The operating system is then able to allocate a system segment table entry and initialise both segment tables appropriately. If a process attempts to access a segment that is not marked as defined, then a program fault condition exists.

(2) Access permission

This is similar to the permission information in the purely segmented system described in chapter 9. Some systems include an addition permission bit to show that the segment is accessible only by the operating system. Other systems cater for several levels of privilege within the machine by allocating several bits for each of the read, write and obey states.

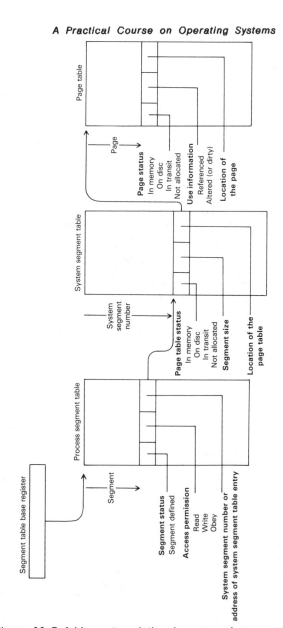

Figure 10.7 Address translation in a paged segmented system

(3) Location of the system segment table entry

This field allows the address translation system to access the system segment table entry that was allocated when the segment was defined. On some machines, where the system segment table begins at a known address, this field might be replaced by a (more compact) system segment number SSN.

10.4.3 System segment table

The system segment table has three fields, as follows:

(1) Page table status

This indicates the position of the page table. In general, four options are possible: the page table could be in memory, on the disc, in transit between the disc and memory or, if the segment has not previously been accessed, space might not have been allocated for it.

(2) Segment size

This is examined by the address translation hardware to check for accesses beyond the defined size of the segment.

(3) Location of the page table

Depending on the status, this field contains the address of the page table either in memory or on the backing store.

10.4.4 Page table

The page table has a status field and location field similar to those in the segment table, except that they relate to the status of the pages in a segment rather than the page table. The third field contains information about the usage of the page. In general, this will be updated whenever a current page register is loaded for the page. If the attempted access is for reading, the referenced bit will be set. If a write access is attempted, both the referenced and altered bits will be set.

10.4.5 Loading of current page registers

The current page registers for this system are shown in figure 10.8. Whenever a location is addressed that is not mapped by the current page registers, the address translation hardware accesses the segment and page tables to find the location of the required page. The sequence for loading a register goes through the following stages:

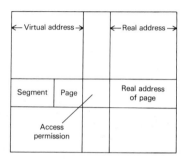

Figure 10.8 Current page registers

(1) Compare the segment field of the virtual address with the limit given in the segment table base register. Generate a program fault interrupt if the limit is exceeded.

(2) Index into the process segment table with the segment number and examine the status field. Generate a program fault interrupt if the segment is undefined.

(3) Save the access permission from the process segment table for subsequent loading into a current page register.

(4) Access the system segment table entry corresponding to this segment and check that the attempted access is within the defined size of the segment. Generate a program fault interrupt if the address is illegal.

(5) If the page table status does not show that the page table is in memory, then generate a virtual store interrupt to retrieve the page table.

(6) Access the page table entry corresponding to the required page. If the page status does not show that the page is in memory, then generate a virtual store interrupt to retrieve the page.

(7) Load a current page register with (a) the segment and page fields of the virtual address, (b) the access permission information retrieved from the process segment table and (c) the location of the page obtained from the page table entry.

(8) Update the usage information in the page table entry according to the type of access attempted.

10.5 ACTION ON A VIRTUAL STORE INTERRUPT

With the sequence described for loading current page registers, all fault conditions that could arise, such as attempting to access an undefined segment or a location beyond the limit of a segment are detected by the address translation hardware. The procedure for servicing virtual store interrupts need not therefore consider these conditions. A typical sequence for servicing the virtual store interrupt is as follows.

10.5.1 Virtual store interrupt procedure

```
Virtual-store-interrupt:
 IF page table is not in store THEN
    bring page table to store      {treat like any other page that is not }
                                   {in store - see note 1                 }

 CASE status of page               {see note 2                           }
    not-previously-accessed:       {pages only allocated when accessed    }
       obtain a page of memory
       clear the page to zero      {set to a predefined value             }
       set page table entry with
          address of page
       return to process
    on-disc:                       {swap page into memory to act as       }
       obtain a page of memory     {destination for the disc transfer     }
       request disc transfer       {disc manager appends to the queue of  }
                                   {pending transfers                     }
       set status in page table
       entry as page in transit
       note process waiting for    {so it can be freed when the transfer  }
       this page                   {is complete                          }
       halt current process
    in-transit:                    {page already being transferred        }
       add process to list of
       others waiting for this page
       halt current process
```

Note 1: The system segment table entry is examined to find the location of the page table. If the page table is not in memory, then steps have to be taken to 'page' it in. If the operating system has been well designed, then transferring in a page table can be performed by the same sequence of code that looks after the transferring in of pages.

Note 2: If the page table is in memory, then the appropriate entry must be inspected to find the status of the required page. This might be:

(a) On the disc.
In this case a free block of memory has to be found into which the page can be transferred, and then a disc transfer is initiated to bring the page into memory. The current process has to be halted until this transfer is completed and a queue of processes waiting for this page is formed, with the current process at its head.

(b) In transit.
If the page is in transit, then it is either being brought into store (at the request of another process) or it is being rejected because it has not been accessed recently. In either case, the only action that can sensibly be performed is to wait until the transfer has been completed. The current process is therefore added to the queue of processes waiting for this page, and then halted.

(c) Not allocated.
In this case, an empty page is acquired and set to some defined state (for example, cleared to zero). The page table is then set to point to the page, and the operating system returns to the process so that it can retry the store access.

10.5.2 Find empty page procedure

In two of the situations above, a free page of memory had to be acquired for the process. This could be performed by the following sequence:

```
Find-empty-page:
  IF no of free pages = 0 THEN
     free store rejection process
     halt current process              {until free space is available }
  Allocate a page in memory
  IF no of free pages < rejection threshold THEN
     free store rejection process      {create free space before it is}
                                        {needed                        }
```

The find empty page routine operates in the following way:

(a) If there are no free pages at all in memory, then the current process has to be halted until space becomes available. The store rejection algorithm is invoked to create some free space.

(b) If there are some free pages, then one can be allocated to the current process. It is potentially a good policy always to monitor a certain amount of free space within the store, so that when a process requests a new page it can be allocated immediately without having to reject a page first. To do this, the find empty page procedure will also trigger the store rejection algorithm whenever the amount of free space falls below a certain threshold (for example, 2 or 4 pages).

10.5.3 Store rejection algorithm

It is often convenient to regard the store rejection operation as an independent operating system process, whose role is to maintain a pool of free space in memory. In order to monitor the usage of each page of memory, an additional table is required for use by the store management system. This table, the memory untilisation table, is illustrated in figure 10.9.

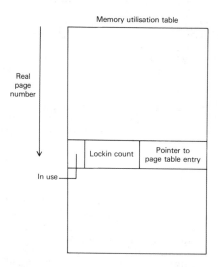

Figure 10.9 Memory utilisation table

For pages that are in use, the entries of the memory utilisation table serve two functions. Part of the entry is a *lockin count* so that a page

can be locked into store and thus ignored by the store rejection
algorithm. For example, a page table would be into store when some of
its pages are also in store, or a page would be locked in if it is
involved in a peripheral transfer. The second part of the entry holds a
pointer back to the corresponding page table entry. This enables the
store rejection algorithm to access the use information in the page table
entry and thus discover if a particular page has been referenced or
altered.

The main action of the store rejection procedure is to transfer pages
out of memory to the backing store. A number of different algorithms
are possible for this, such as first in first out (FIFO), random or least
recently used (LRU); some of these algorithms are described in detail in
chapter 11. The choice of algorithm naturally affects the performance of
the machine. Of these algorithms, least recently used appears to give
the best efficiency, although it is very difficult to implement in practice.
The algorithm shown below is a variant on this and is called the 'not
recently used' algorithm.

```
Store-rejection-process:

REPEAT
    WHILE no of free pages <          {Free a number of pages up to      }
    rejection limit DO                {   the limit                      }
        move pointer to next page     {scan cyclically                   }
        IF page is in use AND         {do not consider free pages or pages }
            page is not locked in THEN {locked in                        }
            IF page has been referenced THEN
                reset the referenced   {do not consider on this scan     }
                information
        ELSE
            remove page from memory   {page not referenced since the last }
                                      {time it was considered            }
    suspend process                   {until store rejection required again}
FOREVER
```

The algorithm relies on scanning the memory utilisation table
cyclically. Naturally, if a page is not in use then it cannot be rejected
(as there is no information to reject). Similarly, a page cannot be
rejected if it is locked in. All other pages are candidates for rejection,
and so a decision is based on the past usage of the page. If the page
has been accessed since the previous time the entry was examined, the
referenced bit will be set in the corresponding page table entry. Such
pages are not good candidates for rejection as they might currently be
in use. The referenced bit is therefore reset and the pointer moved on
to the next page. If a page has not been referenced, then it has been
out of use for at least as long as it has taken to scan around all of the
other pages in store. It is therefore a reasonable candidate to reject.

The act of removing a page normally involves starting a disc transfer to copy the page out. This can be avoided, however, if there is already a copy of the page on the disc, that is the page was transferred in from disc a short time earlier and the copy in store has not been altered (as shown by the usage information in the page table entry). In this situation, the page table entry is immediately set to point to the block on the disc and the page of memory is returned to the pool of free space.

10.5.4 Disc interrupt procedure

Disc transfers are initiated both by the virtual store interrupt procedure and the store rejection algorithm. On completion of a disc transfer, the disc interrupt procedure has to update the operating system tables according to the type of transfer. This involves:

(1) For transfers from store to disc (that is rejection transfers), the block of memory is marked as free and any programs waiting for space are freed (see the find empty page procedure).
(2) The page table entry is set to point to the page at its new location.
(3) Any programs that are waiting for this page (having generated a virtual store interrupt when it was on the disc or in transit) are then freed.
(4) Finally, the interrupt procedure will start up the next transfer if there are any more entries in the disc transfer queue.

10.6 REFERENCES

J. K. Buckle (1978). *The ICL2900 Series*, Macmillan, London.

R. C. Daley and J. B. Dennis (1968). 'Virtual memory, processes, and sharing in MULTICS', *Communications of the ACM*, Vol. 11, pp. 306–12.

D. B. G. Edwards, A. E. Knowles and J. V. Woods (1981). 'MU6G: A new design to achieve mainframe performance from a mini-sized computer', *ACM 7th Annual Symposium on Computer Architecture*, May 1980.

T. Kilburn, D. B. G. Edwards, M. J. Lanigan and F. H. Sumner (1962). 'One-level storage system', *IRE Transactions on Electronic Computers EC11*, Vol. 2, pp. 223–235.

T. Kilburn, D. Morris, J. S. Rohl and F. H. Sumner (1968). 'A system design proposal', *Proceedings of the IFIP Conference, Edinburgh*, 1968.

10.7 PROBLEMS

1. Explain how storage protection is achieved for a virtual storage system in a paged machine.

2. Explain the mapping of virtual addresses to real addresses in a paged segmented machine.

3. Compare and contrast the principles of paging and segmentation.

4. Explain how the performance of a paged computer varies during the course of running a single job and when a number of jobs are multiprogrammed. What techniques might be used by the operating system to maintain good performance?

5. Outline table structures appropriate to the management of the following kinds of paging systems:

   (a) a system with a small number of fixed size pages (say, < 500)
   (b) a system with a large number of fixed size pages (say, > 5000)
   (c) a system with variable-sized pages.

   Discuss in particular what information might be contained in these structures to assist the page-rejection algorithms.

11 Memory Management – Algorithms and Performance

11.1 PERFORMANCE

The previous three chapters have discussed the development of the memory management systems leading to a paging system. The performance of a paging system will now be considered.

The performance of a program varies considerably with the number of pages that it has in store. On entering a process, because there are very few pages in store, relatively few instructions can be obeyed before there is a virtual store interrupt. If it is possible to have all of a program and its data in store, then no virtual store interrupts occur. The behaviour of a program can be summarised as shown in figure 11.1.

Between points A and B, the performance of the machine is extremely poor. However, on approaching point B, the pages most frequently used by the program are in store and so the performance of the machine improves dramatically. The number of pages for which this happens in known as the *working set*. The working set varies between programs, and between different phases in the execution of a program (for example, editing, compiling, running).

Between points B and C, the performance continues to improve but at a much more gradual rate. At point C, all of the program is in store and so there are no more virtual store interrupts.

If there are a number of programs in store together, as might happen in multiprogramming in a time-sharing system, it is difficult to decide how much store each program should be allowed to occupy. Sufficient space to hold the whole program (point C) could be allocated, but this might be very large indeed. In practice, the performance of the machine will be satisfactory as long as a program has its working set

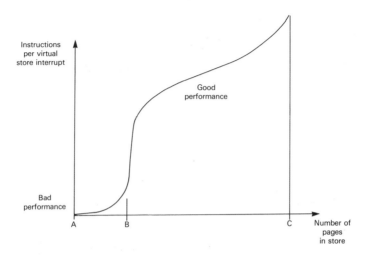

Figure 11.1 Performance of a paging system

available. This will generally be considerably less than the total program size.

If a process does not have all of its pages in store, there will be periods when pages have to be transferred in from the backing store. During this period other processes can be multiprogrammed, so that the central processor is kept busy. The CPU utilisation therefore varies according to the graph in figure 11.2.

Up to point D, the utilisation is improving as the level of multiprogramming increases. However, when point D is reached, a situation such as the following occurs

Program 1 requests a page from backing store.
        This triggers store rejection which decides to reject a page of program 2.

Multiprogramming occurs and program 2 is run.

Program 2 requests a page from backing store.
        This triggers store rejection which decides to reject a page of program 1.
    etc.

The resulting situation is that no program has its working set in store

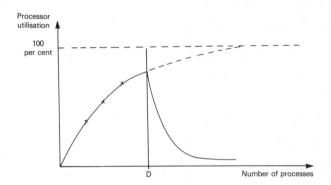

Figure 11.2 CPU utilisation

and in consequence the performance falls off dramatically. This unstable state is known as *thrashing*, when the performance might drop down to a few per cent (for example, 5-10 per cent or less). To ensure good performance:

$$\sum_{1}^{N} \text{WORKING SETS} \leq \text{STORE SIZE}$$

The effect of thrashing will be described in greater detail later in this chapter.

Virtual memory organisations such as paging make possible the running of programs whose total store requirement is greater than the available store size. When this is done, there is inevitably a deterioration in performance because of servicing page faults and it is essential to remember that, beyond a certain point, paging is no substitute for real memory. Failure to acknowledge this fact results in programs (and sometimes systems) whose execution speed depends on the disc speed rather than the store speed. For example, with a 100 ns instruction time and a 5 ms page fault time, 50,000 instructions must be obeyed between page faults to get even 50 per cent utilisation of the processor.

One of the limiting factors on the rate at which work can be processed in a time-sharing system is the time taken to swap jobs to and from main store. Consider a typical interactive editing activity. The swap time might be the time taken to page in, say, eight 1 Kbyte pages, or

$$8 * (\text{average latency} + \text{page transfer time})$$

If the average latency is 5 ms, and the page transfer time is 0.5 ms, this gives a swap time of 44 ms. Had the job been swapped in as a single unit, the time would have been

$$1 * \text{average latency} + 8 * \text{page transfer time}$$

or 9 ms. Obviously this extension of swap times by a factor of 5 or more is not acceptable.

If the page size is increased, then clearly more information is fetched to store for each transfer (and hence for each latency time). Thus, provided that the extra data fetched is actually useful, performance can be improved in this way. On the other hand if the extra information turns out not to be required, then time has been wasted in fetching it to store and (more importantly) it has occupied more store than necessary. So, for example, fetching eight 1 Kbyte pages would take:

$$8 * (\text{average latency} + \text{page transfer time}) = 44 \text{ ms}$$

while fetching four 2 Kbyte pages would take

$$4 * (\text{average latency} + 2 \text{ page transfer time}) = 24 \text{ ms}$$

Inherent in a paging system is the need for a page table that is available for access. This produces an additional overhead requirement not needed in an unpaged system.

Obviously, if the page size is increased, then the overhead increases, but on the other hand the number of pages per segment (and hence page table size) decreases. Thus a compromise must be made to produce a page size that gives reasonably optimal utilisation.

An alternative consideration would be to have a store hierarchy of more than the two levels so far described. For example, there might be several main memories and backing stores, differing in capacity and speed and different page sizes might be chosen for each of the different levels. Clearly many configurations are possible within such a system, but consider the following case with three levels of store

(1) Disc
(2) Mass Core (large but slow)
(3) Small Core (fast but very limited capacity).

It is advantageous to transfer larger pages between the disc and the mass store than between the mass and small core. If a mass page size of 4 Kbytes is used and a small core page size of 1 Kbyte, then the time to fetch four consecutive 1 Kbyte pages from disc to small memory is:

(1 * disc -> mass transfer) + (4 * mass -> small core transfer)

= (1 * average latency + 4 Kbyte transfer time)
+ (4 * 1 Kbyte transfer time)

= (5 + 2) + (4 * 0.5) = 9 ms

On the other hand, if we transferred directly from disc to small core in 1 Kbyte pages the time would be:

4 * (average latency + page transfer time)
= 22 ms

So, by using a different page size at the two levels, transfer times can be by a factor 22/9. This is clearly the optimal case for these page sizes, as all the pages transferred to mass are eventually used. In the worst case, only one of the four pages is actually used, so the time would be:

(1 * disc -> mass transfer) + (1 * mass -> small transfer)

= (1 * average latency + 4 Kbyte transfer time)
+ (1 * 1 Kbyte transfer time)

= (5 + 2) + (1 * 0.5) = 8 ms

whereas, with direct 1 Kbyte transfers from disc to small memory:

(1 * disc -> small transfer) = (average latency + 1 Kbyte transfer)
= 5.5 ms

Hence, in the worst case the performance decreases by a factor of 8/5.5 as a result of using two page sizes. Note, though, that the extra space wasted is in mass rather than the small memory.

11.2 LOCALITY.

The fact that reasonable performance can be achieved with programs greater than store size is due to the phenomenon, defined in chapter 9, known as *locality*. This can be described informally as a tendency by programs to cluster their page references, and leads to the typical curve for number of page faults against store size for a program shown in figure 11.3.

Clearly, even for a very large store, there will be a certain minimum number of page faults to get the pages into memory initially. Once the pages are all in memory the program runs with no further page faults.

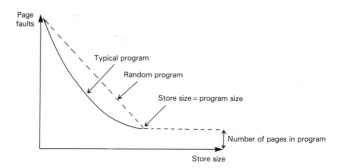

Figure 11.3 Page faults against store size

For store sizes less than the program size, more page faults may occur as a result of rejecting a page that is subsequently needed again. However, the number of page faults does not increase linearly with decreasing store size, as some pages that are rejected may never be used again. This is a consequence of locality. A program accessing its pages randomly would tend to give a much worse performance (more page faults) for a given store size than typical real programs, as illustrated by figure 11.3.

In a time-sharing system, similar remarks can be made about each interaction. At the start of its time slice, a job will tend to have all its pages on backing store and will therefore need to fetch to store the pages used in the time slice. The number of extra page faults then depends on the amount of store available to it, which might be the real store size or the amount of space allocated to it by the operating system.

In principle, locality can be treated as two separate interacting phenomena – *temporal* and *spatial* locality. Temporal locality refers to the high probability of a page that has just been accessed being accessed again soon. Spatial locality refers to the high probability that, if a page is accessed, the adjacent pages will be accessed soon. Both phenomena tend to arise naturally as a result of normal programming practice, and programmers can often greatly improve the performance of their programs by packing procedures and data that are used at the same time physically close together in the store.

From the point of view of the operating system, temporal and spatial locality are not particularly useful concepts, and locality is normally treated as a single phenomenon formalised in the *Working Set* concept. The working set of a program at a given instant is the set of pages it needs in store at that instant:

WS(t, τ) = {pages accessed in the interval [t, t + τ]}

In practice this set is not usually known by the operating system, but as a result of locality it is very well approximated for small intervals by

WS(t, τ) = {pages accessed in the interval [t − τ, t]}

Often only the number of pages required is of interest (so that a sensible amount of space can be allocated) and so the working set size is defined as:

WSS(t, τ) = number of pages in WS(t, τ)

Intuitively, the working set is the number of pages needed by a job to run reasonably efficiently, so values of τ must be such that a few page requests can be afforded. For example, values of $\tau \geqslant 50,000$ instructions might be reasonable. For a batch job, the working set might typically be around half the total job size; for an interactive job, the total number of pages accessed during a (short) time slice is a good estimate.

11.3 PAGE REPLACEMENT ALGORITHMS

When a program is run in a small store, its performance will depend to some extent on the algorithm used to reject pages from memory, that is, the replacement algorithm. Once again it is necessary to stress that, if the store is excessively small, even the best replacement algorithm cannot give good performance. For reasonable performance, the store size must be at least as big as the program's working set size. The objective of the replacement algorithm is then to choose a page to replace that which is not in the program's working set. (Note that for the time being only a system running a single job is being considered. The effects of multiprogramming will be considered later.)

The following page replacement algorithms will now be considered:

    (1) The Belady optimal replacement (BO)
    (2) Least recently used (LRU)
    (3) First in first out (FIFO)
    (4) Not recently used (NRU)

11.3.1 Belady Optimal Replacement Algorithm (BO)

This is mentioned mainly for historical reasons since the first conclusive study of page replacement algorithms was made by Belady in 1966. Several algorithms were studied by simulations, and a replacement algorithm was presented and proved optimal. The algorithm is:

> 'replace the page which will not be needed again for the
> longest time'.

This corresponds to trying to keep the job's working set in memory.
However it is not a very practical algorithm as normally it is not known
what the future reference pattern will be. Its main use is therefore as a
reference point relative to which other algorithms can be assessed. It
has proved useful in compiler optimisation, as an algorithm for register
allocation, where the future reference pattern is known in advance.

11.3.2 Least Recently Used Algorithm (LRU)

The phenomenon of program locality means that a programs working set
varies slowly with time. Thus the immediate past reference history usually
serves as a good predictor for the immediate future, and an excellent
approximation to the BO algorithm is:

> 'replace the page which has been used least recently'

That is, the page that has been out of use the longest. This is the
least recently used algorithm, and in practice it has been shown to
perform well.

The problem with LRU is that it is still difficult to implement; a true
LRU implementation requires that the hardware maintain an indication of
'time since last use' for each store page. Without such hardware
assistance, the choice of algorithm is effectively limited (for efficiency
reasons) to those that use information obtained at page fault times −
that is, it is impractical to place a software overhead on every page
access, and therefore information can be gathered only during the (it is
hoped) infrequent page faults.

The worst case for LRU rejection (and indeed for all 'sensible'
non−lookahead algorithms) is a program that accesses its pages
cyclically in a store that is not large enough. For example, the trace of
store accesses

$$(0, 1024, 2048, 3072, 4096, 0, 1024, 2048...)$$

in a 4 Kbyte store with 1 Kbyte page size gives a page fault for every
reference. The reason that the common case of cyclic accessing is so
bad for many replacement algorithms is obvious if an attempt is made to
apply the BO algorithm to it. This shows that the optimal choice for
rejection in this case is always the *most recently accessed* page, which
is contrary to expectations from the locality principle. (Obviously,
programs with cyclic access patterns exhibit very poor temporal locality.)

11.3.3 First In First Out Algorithm (FIFO).

The FIFO algorithm is quite commonly used as it is very easy to implement. It consists in replacing the page that has been in store the longest. It is not difficult to find intuitive justifications for the choice – a page fetched to store a long time ago may now have fallen out of use. On the other hand it might have been in constant use since it was fetched, in which case it would be a poor replacement choice.

FIFO replacement again performs very badly with cyclic accessing. However, it also exhibits another kind of bad behaviour, known as the FIFO anomaly. For certain page traces, it is possible with FIFO replacement that the number of page faults increases when the store size is increased. Obviously this is a highly undesirable situation. Although an increase in the real store size of a machine is a relatively rare event, the FIFO anomaly could be serious in a paged multiprogramming system. Here the operating system might allocate a 'quota' of store to each job, increasing the size of a job's quota if it suffers too many page faults. The effect of the FIFO anomaly is potentially disastrous.

As an example of the anomaly, consider the page trace

$$(4, 3, 2, 1, 4, 3, 5, 4, 3, 2, 1, 5)$$

running in store of sizes 3 and 4 pages. With a store of size 3 pages, there are 9 page faults:

$$(4^*, 3^*, 2^*, 1^*, 4^*, 3^*, 5^*, 4, 3, 2^*, 1^*, 5)$$

If the store size is increased to 4 pages, there are 10 page faults:

$$(4^*, 3^*, 2^*, 1^*, 4, 3, 5^*, 4^*, 3^*, 2^*, 1^*, 5^*)$$

Note that rejection is on longest time in store without regard to most recent access.

For comparison, the corresponding cases using LRU would give:

For 3 pages store $(4^*,3^*,2^*,1^*,4^*,3^*,5^*,4,3,2^*,1^*,5^*)$ – 10 page faults
For 4 pages store $(4^*,3^*,2^*,1^*,4,3,5^*,4,3,2^*,1^*,5^*)$ – 8 page faults

The existence of such pathological cases gives some cause for worry about the use of algorithms such as FIFO. It will be shown that LRU and BO, and indeed a whole class of algorithms called *stack algorithms* to which they belong, do not exhibit this behaviour. Before doing this, however, we will look at one more commonly used replacement algorithm.

11.3.4 Not Recently Used Algorithm (NRU)

The NRU algorithm tries to partition the pages in store into two groups: those that have been used 'recently', and those that have not. It then rejects any page that has not been used recently. The most common implementation consists of a FIFO replacement algorithm, modified to give recently used pages a second chance. It operates as follows:

> Whenever a page is accessed, it is marked as 'referenced'. (This requires hardware support, but is fairly inexpensively achieved, and is included in most paging hardware.) When it is required to reject a page, a cyclic scan of the pages in store is made (as in the FIFO algorithm). If the page being considered is not marked as 'referenced', it is rejected as usual. If it marked as 'referenced', it is altered to 'not referenced', and the reject algorithm moves on to consider the next page. Next time this page is considered it will be marked 'not referenced' unless it has been accessed again in the meantime.

Obviously this algorithm is easy to implement – almost as easy as the simple FIFO algorithm – and gives an approximation to the LRU algorithm. Consequently, it tends to give better performance than straightforward FIFO. However, it does still suffer from the FIFO anomaly for some page traces (not necessarily the same page traces as for FIFO though).

The NRU idea can be generalised to give a closer approximation to LRU by partitioning into more than two groups and rejecting from the 'least recently used' group. The easiest way to do this is to associate a counter with each page. Whenever the page is referenced, the counter is set to some value x. Each time a page is considered for rejection, its counter is decremented and the page is rejected only when the counter falls to zero. Obviously, the value of x needs careful tuning since if it is too high, many redundant passes will be made through the list of pages before finally deciding on a suitable candidate to reject. It is possible over a period of time to adjust x to obtain the optimum spread of pages into groups such that there are always pages available in the 'zero' (replaceable) group.

11.4 STACK ALGORITHMS

Although it may not arise frequently, the FIFO anomaly is somewhat worrying in the context of multiprogramming systems, where it can defeat attempts to calculate optimal store allocations for jobs. There is therefore interest in defining algorithms that do not exhibit anomalous behaviour. A class of algorithms known as *stack algorithms*, of which both LRU and BO are members, can be shown not to suffer from the FIFO anomaly. A stack algorithm is defined as follows:

> Let S(A, P, k, N) be the set of pages in store when processing reference k of the page trace P using replacement algorithm A in a store of size N pages

> Then A is a stack algorithm if, for all P, k, and N:

$$S(A, P, k, N) \leqslant S(A, P, k, N + 1)$$

That is, if the store size is increased, then at any instant in time the same set of pages are in store as for the smaller size, plus possibly some more. Obviously if this is satisfied it is not possible to suffer more page faults with the larger store size.

It is very easy to show that both LRU and BO are, indeed, stack algorithms. For

S(LRU, P, k, N)   = the last N   distinct pages referenced in P
S(LRU, P, k, N + 1) = the last N + 1 distinct pages referenced in P

and quite clearly, S(LRU, P, k, N) ≤ S(LRU, P, k, N + 1). Similarly

S(BO, P, k, N)   = the next N   distinct pages referenced in P
S(BO, P, k, N + 1) = the next N + 1 distinct pages referenced in P

and therefore S(BO, P, k, N) ≤ S(BO, P, k, N + 1)

11.5 MULTIPROGRAMMING

So far only the effects of paging for a single user have been considered. However, a system capable of supporting multiprogramming is required and the existence of such a requirement imposes new criteria on the paged system. It has already been noted that the time taken to 'swap-in' a job in a demand paging system (that is, to fetch its working set to store) can be much greater than the time for a job of equivalent size in an unpaged system because latency costs are incurred on each page transfer rather than just once for the entire job.

The effect of this extended swap time is to increase the 'effective' service times of jobs. In a system where swapping and computing are partially overlapped, the effective service time is max(q, s) where q is the average CPU time used per time slice and s is the swap time. Thus a large increase in s tends to make s ≫ q, and so the response time for a given number of users increases drastically. (Conversely, the number of users who can be serviced with a given response time falls.)

Clearly, the factor that limits response times is 'number of jobs swapped per second', rather than the swap time for individual jobs, though the two are related. This means that one of two main strategies can be adopted to improve performance:

(1) Reduce the time taken to swap individual jobs.
(2) Improve the swap rates by swapping in more than one job at once.

11.5.1 Reducing Individual Swap Times – Prepaging

To reduce individual job swap times, the latency that occurs between page transfers must somehow be eliminated or at least reduced. One approach might be to try to place the pages of a job on the backing store in such a way that these latencies were minimised. This is very difficult since it is not usually possible to predict the precise sequence and timing of page transfers, and hence to know where pages are to be placed. (However, with moving-head devices (discs) it certainly *does* pay to try to keep all the pages of a job together, so as to minimise seek times.)

The difficulty mentioned above is a result of using demand paging, so the job itself determines the order in which pages are requested and the timing of the requests. A more effective stategy is therefore to try to prefetch a job's pages without waiting for them to be demanded. In general this is not possible; but at the start of the time slice it is known that a job will have to fetch its working set to memory. Furthermore, a reasonable estimate can be made about which pages are in the working set, by noting which ones were accessed during the previous time slice. If, before running a job, the system arranges to prefetch its working set to memory, the order in which the pages are to be fetched can be determined so as to reduce latencies. This may or may not be coupled with judicious placement of pages on the backing store but, even without this a better performance would be expected just from scheduling transfers in the optimum sequence.

11.5.2 Improving Swap Rates By Multiprogramming

The disadvantage of prepaging is, of course, that it can result in many redundant page transfers when a job changes its working set. This happens for example if a user switches to a new kind of activity or even if his job switches to a new phase. So, there is some attraction in devising efficient policies that still make use of demand paging.

As already observed, the requirement is for the operating system to have some control over the order in which page transfers are serviced. This is not possible for a single job under demand paging. However, with many jobs, if each has a page request outstanding, choice can be made to service these in a sequence that minimises latencies. (In practice of course, the page requests are serviced as they occur and transfer requests are passed on to the disc manager. It is the disc manager that maintains a queue of outstanding transfer requests and chooses which to service next.)

The following is one way of organising such a system. The coordinator maintains a list of processes in the current 'multiprogramming mix' (which may be a subset of all the jobs in the system) in priority order. Whenever the highest priority process is halted, the next is entered, and so on. Whenever any process completes its time slice it is moved to the end of the list, and all the processes beneath it move up one place.

The effect of this strategy is as follows. It is hoped that, by the time a process reaches the top priority position, its working set is in memory. Whenever it suffers a page fault (infrequently) the next job is entered, and so on. Between them, the top few jobs are able to use most of the processor time. Whenever one of the jobs lower down the queue is entered, it is likely to suffer an immediate page fault as it has not yet established its working set in memory. This causes the next process to be entered, make an immediate page request,... and so on. The overall effect is that a number of page requests are generated in very rapid succession and the system can then service these in an optimum sequence. Thus several jobs are being swapped simultaneously. The effect on performance is similar to prepaging, but only pages that are actually required are fetched.

The scheme has two main disadvantages as compared with prepaging. The first is that a larger quantity of store is needed. For a prepaging system, only enough space for two jobs is needed: one running and the other being prepaged. If multiprogramming several jobs, then enough storage space for all of them must be available. The second disadvantage applies only to systems that use a moving-head device as a backing store. Since pages are being fetched for several different processes at once, there is a much higher probability that successive page requests will be on different tracks and thus will incur seek overheads as well as rotational latency.

11.6 THRASHING

When several processes are multiprogrammed in a paging system, it was shown that a phenomenon known as thrashing can occur. Thrashing is an instability that arises when the total store requirements of the jobs being multiprogrammed exceeds the available main memory size. As an example, consider two jobs A and B, accessing 4 pages each in a memory of size 7 pages. A possible sequence of events is as follows:

```
A accesses page A1;   page fault;   A halted
B accesses page B1;   page fault;   B halted
A accesses page A2;   page fault;   A halted
B accesses page B2;   page fault;   B halted
A accesses page A3;   page fault;   A halted
B accesses page B3;   page fault;   B halted
A accesses page A4;   page fault;   A halted
B accesses page B4;   page fault;   A1 rejected;   B halted
A accesses page A1;   page fault;   B1 rejected;   A halted
B accesses page B1;   page fault;   A2 rejected;   B halted
etc.
```

The overall effect is that almost no useful instructions are executed. Either job would run alone with almost 100 per cent efficiency; when they are multiprogrammed in the above way, efficiency drops to only a few percent. This is a very serious problem that has been observed on most paged computing systems. Obviously, the above is an extreme example but it can be said with certainty that if the sum of the working sets of all jobs being multiprogrammed exceeds the available store size, performance will deteriorate to an unacceptable level.

Thrashing is due to interference between jobs being multiprogrammed; that is, each job is continually causing rejection of a page in the working set of one of the others. There are thus two possible approaches to its prevention:

(1) Limit multiprogramming to a 'safe' level — that is, such that the sum of the working sets is less than the store size.

(2) Prevent interference between processes being multiprogrammed.

11.6.1 Thrashing Prevention By Load Control

The approach here is to limit the level of multiprogramming so that all active working sets fit into memory. This applies only to the very rapid multiprogramming that arises for events like page transfers. Very many more processes can still be dealt with by multiprogramming on longer term events such as terminal input/output. Effectively, the coordinator must restrict itself (or be restricted) to a subset; other schedulers such as the process scheduler can still deal with all processes. The total number of jobs in the system is still determined by response time considerations.

Three main forms of load control can be identified for the prevention of thrashing:

(1) Fixed safe multiprogramming level.
(2) Multiprogramming level based on working set estimates.

(3) Multiprogramming level adjusted iteratively, depending on page fault frequency.

The first obviously suffers from an inability to deal with extreme jobs: smaller than average jobs cause space to be wasted, larger than average ones may cause thrashing to occur. This can be offset to some extent in a batch system by giving the operator control over the multiprogramming level, although it is not always easy or convenient for the operator to react quickly to changes in the loading.

If the system can make an estimate of a job's working set size by monitoring its page references, then these estimates can be used to control multiprogramming, by considering only jobs such that the sum of their working sets fit into memory. In a time-sharing system, a suitable estimate may be the number of pages referenced in the previous time slice. This method operates well in conjunction with the prepaging strategies discussed earlier.

Finally it is possible to adjust the level of multiprogramming automatically, effectively by trying to detect thrashing when it begins to occur. This is done by monitoring the frequency of page faults: if they occur too often the multiprogramming level is reduced, if they occur with less than a certain threshold frequency it is increased. The main problem here is that individual jobs with very bad paging characteristics can have a disastrous effect on the multiprogramming level.

11.6.2 Thrashing Prevention By Controlling Interference

The interference that causes thrashing is brought about when one process causes pages in the working set of another to be rejected from store. This form of interference can be prevented by controlling the extent to which processes may reject one another's pages.

Most systems operate by assigning a *quota* of pages (possibly based on working set estimates) to each process, such that all quotas fit into memory. Each process is then allowed to reject pages of others until it has its quota of store pages; after this it may be allowed to take further pages if they are free, but if rejection becomes necessary it is forced to reject one of its own pages. Thus the replacement algorithm is required to operate *locally* within each process rather than globally on all processes in the system. This is clearly a sensible policy since the majority of replacement algorithms are designed to take advantage of the reference properties of individual jobs. Obviously there are many variants, depending on exactly *how* the quotas are assigned (by compilers, users, operators or automatically by the system) and what algorithm is used for rejection.

There are also strategies that do not involve explicitly assigning quotas, of which the following is fairly typical. The processes are ordered in the multiprogramming mix according to their relative priorities and an indication is kept with each page of the priority of its owning process. Then, processes are allocated to reject pages of processes at their own and lower priority levels, but never of higher priority ones. Clearly this prevents thrashing. However, it does tend to result in an accumulation of little-used pages for the higher priority processes, and it has been suggested that store utilisation is improved by choosing a random page at intervals and rejecting it.

It should be noted that these policies are designed to prevent the total collapse of performance as a result of thrashing. Individual jobs may still perform very badly if they are too large for the quotas assigned, but at least they do not cause other, well-behaved jobs to suffer. Thus overall system utilisation may be quite high even in the presence of one or two badly behaved jobs.

11.7 STORAGE ALLOCATION TECHNIQUES

The allocation of storage also presents a major problem to the designer of memory management systems, and it is also an area in which many different algorithms are currently in use. The choice of a suitable allocation strategy is not just appropriate for the allocation of main memory but also for the allocation of space on the backing store, and in general, a system may use different algorithms for each level in the storage hierarchy.

Inevitably, the choice of algorithm involves a compromise, and in this case the aim is to achieve the most effective utilisation of the store while at the same time performing the allocation efficiently. The 'efficiency' of the technique is assessed in terms of the speed with which an area of store can be allocated and in terms of the space occupied by the data structures needed to monitor the usage of the store. When large backing stores are considered, this latter aspect can be particularly crucial.

In general, the allocation of space on a paged machine is considerably simpler than on a purely segmented machine. As all the pages in memory are of equal size, it is largely irrelevant as to which is allocated whenever a new page is required. The emphasis therefore is on using the fastest technique for performing the allocation, as any page chosen is equally good. As was seen in chapter 9, the situation is not as simple with segmented machines. Fragmentation can have a significant effect on the utilisation of the memory, and as a consequence, degrade the overall efficiency and throughput of the system.

The choice of data structures for monitoring the usage of the store is largely determined by the characteristics of the storage medium concerned. Two main techniques are used; (a) a linked list, where free blocks are chained together using the first few locations of each block to hold the size and linkage information, and (b) a bit vector, where each bit corresponds to a block of a certain unit size and indicates whether the block is free or allocated. In this case, larger areas than the unit size are allocated by searching for multiple consecutive free blocks. The first technique is really only applicable to the allocation of space in the main memory, as it is inpractical to chain together free blocks on a disc.

The most common techniques for performing the allocation of store are known as (a) the first fit algorithm, (b) the next fit algorithm, (c) the best fit algorithm, (d) the worst fit algorithm and (e) a buddy system. Their principles are outlined below, and they are examined in more detail by Knuth (1973). No technique should be regarded as universally the 'best' as each can be effective under different circumstances.

11.7.1 First fit algorithm

With this technique, the list of free blocks (or the bit vector) is scanned until a block of at least the required size is found. The block is allocated with any excess space being returned to the pool of free blocks. Each time a new block is required, the search is started from the beginning of the list. The effect of this is that small blocks are more readily allocated at the start of memory, whereas more of the list has to be scanned if the store is relatively full or if larger areas are required.

11.7.2 Next fit algorithm

This technique, also known as the modified first fit algorithm, operates in a similar way to the first fit technique except that whenever a block is required, the search is started from the point reached the previous time. It is, in effect, a cyclic scan of the list of free blocks. As a consequence, there is a more even distribution in the allocation of storage, normally with lower search times. However, it has a higher potential for failing to allocate a block due to fragmentation.

11.7.3 Best fit algorithm

This technique allocates the block closest to the required size. Inevitably it involves scanning the entire list of free blocks (unless a block of the *exact* size is found before reaching the end). It is therefore quite costly in terms of the time spent searching the data structures, although it produces a good utilisation of the store.

11.7.4 Worst fit algorithm

A criticism of the best fit algorithm is that the space remaining after allocating a block of the required size is so small that in general it is of no real use. The worst fit algorithm therefore allocates space from the block which will leave the largest portion of free space. The hope is that this will be large enough to satisfy another request. It has the disadvantage, however, that the largest blocks are allocated first and so a request for a large area is more likely to fail.

11.7.5 Buddy system

The buddy system operates by allocating space in a limited number of sizes, for example, powers of 2 of the minimum block size. A separate list is kept of the blocks of each size, thus allocating a block merely involves removing a block from the appropriate list. If the list is empty, a block of the next larger size is split in order to satisfy the request, and the excess space is relinked on to the list of the appropriate size. When space is released, the block is linked into the appropriate free list, but if it is found that the adjacent blocks (its buddies) are also free, then these may be combined to form a free block of the next larger size.

This scheme is effective in that allocation of space is fast, but it does not necessarily produce the optimal utilisation of the store due to the restriction of only allocating space in a limited number of sizes.

11.8 REFERENCES

L. A. Belady (1966). 'A Study of Replacement Algorithms for a Virtual-storage Computer'. *IBM Systems Journal*, Vol. 5, pp. 78–101.

P. Calingaert (1967). 'System Performance Evaluation: Survey and Appraisal', *Communications of the ACM*, Vol. 10, pp. 12–8.

D. E. Knuth (1973). *The Art of Computer Programming, Volume 1 Fundamental Algorithms*, Addison-Wesley, Reading, Mass..

H. Lucas (1971). 'Performance Evaluation and Monitoring', *ACM Computing Surveys*, Vol. 3, pp. 79–91.

W. C. Lynch (1972). 'Operating System Performance', *Communication of the ACM*, Vol. 15, pp. 579–85.

11.9 PROBLEMS

1. Discuss how some processes can behave better under the implementation of different page replacement algorithms.

2. Discuss the reasons why a program that has good locality would expect to have good efficiency for its execution.

3. Describe the phenomenon of thrashing, and explain why a global page replacement policy is more susceptible to thrashing than a local page replacement policy.

4. Discuss the effect of virtual store interrupts on the performance of a paged machine.

12 File Management

Most users of a computer use the facilities of the file system without being aware of the complexity that lies behind it. In general, this complexity does not result because of the nature of the facilities provided, rather because of the need to ensure the security and integrity of the file system. Before examining this rather complex aspect of system design, the fundamental characteristics of a file system will be examined. In principle, the facilities that are expected of a file system are quite simple. The following would be a fairly typical set:

(1) To be able to create and delete files.

(2) To be able to control access to the files, such as by preventing a data file from being obeyed.

(3) To be able to refer to files by symbolic name, and not to worry about the precise location of the files on the backing store.

(4) To be able to share files.

(5) To be able to list the files currently owned by a user.

(6) To have the files protected against failure of the operating system and/or the hardware.

The system manager might have further requirements, such as:

(7) The ability to introduce new users or delete users and their files from the system.

(8) The ability to introduce new storage media, such as additional

disc packs or magnetic tapes for use by the file system.

In general, the provision of these facilities relies on preserving information about the files on the backing store, and on ensuring the security and integrity of the file system. The following attributes of a file management system are therefore considered in this chapter:

(1) Directories and access rights.

(2) Dumping and archiving.

(3) Security of the file system.

12.2 DIRECTORIES AND ACCESS RIGHTS

The provision of the user facilities tends to revolve around providing a suitable *catalogue* or *directory* of files belonging to each user. Each directory entry contains fields to indicate:

(a) The symbolic name of the file.
(b) The position and size of the file on the backing store.
(c) The access permitted to the file.

Most of the general user requirements can be satisfied by allowing a user to add or delete entries and list the contents of the directory (items 1, 3 and 5). The provision of shared files (item 4) is a much more complex topic and depends largely on the relationship between directories and on maintaining permission information with each directory stating how other users may access the files.

In many respects, associating access permission information with each file is of use even for protecting the file from illegal accesses by its *owner*. This permission information is very similar to that described in chapter 9 for segments, as a file may have read, write and obey access permissions. Thus, for example, a text file would have read and write access associated with it, so that when the file is opened it can be edited; a precompiled program would have obey access (or read and obey access) associated with it.

In addition to the permission information which states how a file may be accessed when in use, there may also be permission information stating how the file may be changed. This is of particular significance for users other than the owner of a file, and may state whether a file can be deleted, updated or perhaps renamed.

The structure of the directories and the relationship between them is the main area where file systems tend to differ, and it is also the area that has the most significant effect on the user interface with the file system. Two directory structures will be described here: (a) a single-level directory, and (b) a hierarchical directory.

12.2.1 Single-level directory structure.

In the simplest situation, the system maintains a *master block* that has one entry for each user of the computer. The master block entries contain the address of the individual directories so that, in effect, all directories are at the same level and all users are regarded equally. An example of this type of system is illustrated in figure 12.1.

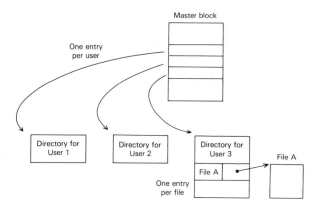

Figure 12.1 Single-level directory structure

When a user logs on to the computer, the directory (and all the files) associated with that user name are available for use. In order to share files one needs to indicate the user who owns the file as well as the file name. Additional protection is often provided when sharing files, either by requiring a password to gain access to the file, or by having the owner provide a list of users who can access the file.

This single-level directory may be adequate in the situation where all users are of equal status, such as a class of students in a laboratory. However in other situations, the environment lends itself to a differential structure of directories which might reflect the nature of the organisation using the computer. One approach to this is provided by the hierarchical directory structure.

12.2.2 Hierarchical directory structure

The primary benefit of having a hierarchical directory structure is that it reflects the management structure within organisations, and therefore facilitates the control of users and their resources. There might also be additional benefits for the higher members in the hierarchy when they wish to access the files of their subordinates. Such a scheme is illustrated in figure 12.2.

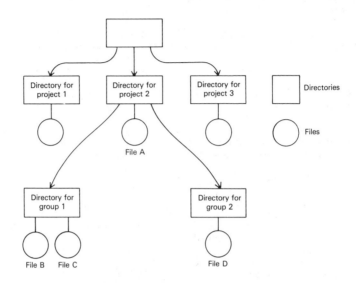

Figure 12.2 Hierarchical directory structure

Here access to files is again made through the appropriate directory; for example, the Group 1 user is able to access the files (File B and File C) under that directory. Access between directories is normally permissible only on a hierarchical basis. Thus, the user Project 2 can gain access to the files under its directory (File A) and to the files in the directories of Group 1 and Group 2. As with the single-level directory structure, restrictions such as password checks may apply if the users Project 1 or Project 3 wish to access these directories or files.

12.3 DUMPING AND ARCHIVING

One of the greatest problems in maintaining a file system is to ensure that the information within the files is not corrupted, either by hardware failure or faults in the system software. A guarantee cannot be given that faults will not occur, and so at least a facility must be available to recover files from earlier versions, should they become corrupt.

The normal way of ensuring that additional copies of a file are maintained is by periodically dumping the file store on to some suitable bulk storage media. For example, a disc may be copied every morning on to a backup disc cartridge. If the disc becomes corrupted during the day, the files as they were at the end of the previous day can be recovered from the backup disc.

This is quite satisfactory where comparatively small amounts of data are involved but, on a very large system, the time to copy the complete file store is prohibitively long. The alternative therefore is to dump only those files that have been altered since the previous dump was taken. This might involve a considerable amount of additional processing to keep track of the latest version of a file across possibly several dump tapes or discs.

Archiving is a facility for deliberately forcing an additional copy of a file to some form of offline media, such as a private disc or tape. This is usually invoked by a user, who wishes either an extra secure version of the file or is wanting some long term storage of the file outside the normal file system.

In some systems it is possible for the operating system to keep a record of when files are used and to invoke automatic file archiving for those which remain unused for long periods. At the same time the user is notified that the relevant files have been archived. Large systems often use this technique to recover file space held by unused files on the fast storage media. Such a technique means that once the archived version is made the original file in the file system is deleted.

Archived files can be restored back into the file system on explicit request, but as the archive media (such as tapes) may have to be mounted on to a peripheral device, there may be a significant delay before the user can gain access to the file.

12.4 SECURE FILE UPDATING

At the beginning of this chapter it was shown that access permission provided a level of file security by stopping a user corrupting a file. Corruption can also occur if faults arise in the hardware or system software, and although dumping and archiving can provide a means of recovering a file once it has been corrupted, it is far better if the files are not corrupted in the first place. There are a number of 'tricks' that the software can use to try to prevent faults occurring.

If we consider, as in figure 12.3 for a single level directory, that the secondary storage contains a master block pointing to directories for each user, which in turn point to the user files, there is a serious problem with the way in which these are updated.

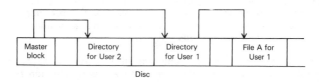

Figure 12.3 File storage system

If File A for User 1 is being updated by overwriting the appropriate area on the disc, and if the machine breaks down while the blocks of the file are being written, it is possible that the area of the disc will contain some blocks of the new File A and some of the old version. This is clearly unsatisfactory as the file is now corrupt. The solution is simply to write the new version to a different area of the disc.

Thus, a new version of File A has now been achieved; the subsequent problem is that the associated file directory has to be updated so that it refers to the new version of File A, and the only secure way of achieving this is to produce a new version of the directory. Similarly, a new version of the master block has to be produced. This corresponds to the situation shown in figure 12.4.

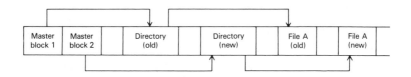

Figure 12.4 File updating system

The question now is: where are the master blocks and how is it possible to distinguish between them? The normal policy is to keep the master blocks at fixed locations on the disc, say at blocks 0 and 1. To distinguish between them, a generation number is kept in the last location of each master block so that when the system is restarted the latest version of the master block (with the last file addition or deletion) is selected. (The last word is used as this should be the very last information transferred to the disc when writing the master blocks.)

The sequence of writing information to the disc is quite crucial for the updating to be secure. The normal sequence is:

(1) Copy the file to the disc – produce *File A (new)*.
(2) Update directory and copy it to the disc – produce *Directory (new)*.
(3) Update master block and copy it to the alternative position on the disc – produce *Master block 2*.

Having completed such a sequence it is possible to recover all the space occupied by the Directory (old) and File A (old). In some systems, however, once File A (new) is created, File A (old) is preserved as a backup version of the file. Any subsequent update then makes the file that is updated the new back-up version and automatically deletes the previous backup version. Such a system is useful during program development since it allows the 'next-most-recent' version to be retained when a file is updated.

In a paged machine, the sequence could be even more complicated, as both the file and the directory could be paged and therefore accessed via a page table. In this case, the sequence adopted could be:

(1) Copy file pages to the disc.
(2) Copy file page table to the disc.
(3) Copy directory pages to the disc.
(4) Copy directory page table to the disc.
(5) Copy the master block to the disc.

12.5 REFERENCES

D. E. Denning and P. J. Denning (1979). 'Data Security', *ACM Computing Surveys*, Vol. 11, pp. 227-49.

12.6 PROBLEMS

1. If a computer system failure occurs it is important to be able to reconstruct a file system quickly and accurately. Explain how this philosophy is achieved for file updating.

2. Discuss the differences between directories based on the single level and hierarchical structures.

3. Discuss the considerations needed to provide adequate backup of files with the difficulties of the overheads of producing the backup versions.

13 Resource Management – Deadlocks

13.1 ALLOCATION OF RESOURCES

One of the major functions of an operating system is to control the resources within the computer system. Indeed, considering CPU time and store as resources, then undoubtedly it is *the* most important function. At a slightly more mundane level, processes need to drive peripherals such as magnetic tape decks or exchangeable disc drives, as users want to mount their own media and have close and dedicated control of the peripherals. In this chapter, the problems of allocating resources to the processes in a multiprogramming system will be examined. As with the allocation of processor time and store, there is a dual objective:

(1) To implement particular management policies regarding which users get the 'best' service.

(2) To optimise the performance of the system.

The first of these is somewhat outside the scope of this book and so only the second objective will be discussed.

Resource allocation is essentially a scheduling problem: whenever a process requests a resource, a decision must be made on whether to allocate it immediately or to make the process wait. The progress of a process from its creation to its termination can thus be regarded as a number of phases, where the process takes control of some resources and subsequently relinquishes control, as illustrated in figure 13.1.

This case is considering a hypothetical system in which input and output devices are under the control of user processes. The major problems with resource allocation arise when several processes are concurrently requesting control of the same resources. For simplicity, consider just two processes, P1 and P2.

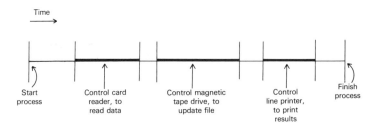

Figure 13.1 Progress of a process during execution

A resource R1 is assumed to be required by both processes at the same time. Clearly this is not possible, as it is assumed that the resources are such that a single process needs exclusive access to a resource. (Imagine a situation where two processes are simultaneously trying to drive the lineprinter.) The first process to request control of the resource is therefore granted control until it is subsequently released. If the second process requests control during this period, it will be halted until the resource becomes available.

The main problem arises when there are two resources, R1 and R2, available. Consider the following sequence:

P1   P2

Obtain (R2)   Obtain (R1)

Obtain (R1) and halt waiting
for P2 to release R1

                                            Obtain (R2) and halt waiting
                                            for P1 to release R2

This is a situation known as a *deadlock* or *deadly embrace*, when neither process can run because each is waiting for a resource under the control of the other process.

13.2 DEADLOCKS

There are five conditions or criteria that, when satisfied, indicate the occurence of a deadlock.

(1) The processes involved must be *irreversible* and thus unable to reset

to an earlier time before they had control of the resources.

(2) Each process must have *exclusive control* of its resources.

(3) There must be *non-preemption* of resources, so that a resource is never released until a process has completely finished with it.

(4) *Resource waiting* must be allowed, so that one process can hold a resource while waiting for another.

(5) There must be a *circular chain* of processes, with each holding resources requested by the next in the chain.

The operating system needs to take explicit action to deal with possible deadlocks. Policies for dealing with deadlocks can be broadly classified as:

(1) Prevention – deadlocks cannot occur because restrictions have been placed on the use of resources.

(2) Detection – deadlocks are detected after they have arisen and action is taken to rectify the matter.

(3) Avoidance – a 'safe' allocation policy is employed and so deadlocks are anticipated and avoided.

13.2.1 Deadlock prevention

Deadlocks may be prevented by placing restrictions on the use of resources such that one or more of the necessary conditions for a deadlock cannot occur. The necessary conditions are:

(1) The resources concerned cannot be shared. This might be achieved by denying the user access to the real, unshareable resources and providing instead a set of 'virtual' resources – for example, spooling achieves this for devices such as lineprinters. However, this cannot be done satisfactorily in all cases – for example, with devices such as magnetic tape and disc drives, the volume of data transferred precludes any attempt at large scale buffering.

(2) The resources cannot be preempted from the processes holding them. If preemption is possible, then the resources could be reallocated and hence the deadlock resolved, but there are obvious examples where preemption would not be acceptable (for example, a file that has already been half updated on the disc).

(3) Processes hold the resources already allocated while waiting

for new ones. One way to avoid this is to allocate all resources at the beginning of a job so that a process does not hold any resources while it is waiting. This is often a reasonable strategy, though it is wasteful for jobs that require certain resources only for short periods of time, and even more so if some resources may not be needed at all (for example, a lineprinter needed only to print an error report if the job goes wrong). A variation that partly gets around this is to allow a job to *release* all its resources, then make a fresh request.

(4) A circular chain of processes exists, each process holding a resource required by the next in the chain. This can be avoided by numbering the various resources types and introducing the rule that a process that holds resource k can request only resources numbered ⩾ k. Obviously the disadvantages are the same as mentioned in (3) above, but a suitable numbering of resource types with commonly used resources given low numbers can greatly reduce the wastage of resources.

The main resources for which none of the above methods is particularly appropriate are files. Read-only files are clearly shareable, but if files are being altered then, except in specialised situations, the above strategies cannot be used.

13.2.2 Deadlock detection

If none of the above methods of deadlock prevention is suitable, then an attempt could be made to *detect* deadlocks when they occur, and resolve the conflict in some way. Deadlock detection operates by detecting the 'circular wait' condition described in (4) above, and so any algorithm for detecting cycles in directed graphs can be used. This can be done using the following data structures:

(1) For each process, a list of the resources it holds.

(2) For each resource, a list of the processes that are waiting for it, and an indication of which process is actually using it.

A check for deadlock can be made at each resource request, (or less frequently, depending on how likely it is to arise). Checking on each request has the advantage of early detection, but on the other hand, less frequent checks consume less processor time and may therefore be preferable. If deadlocks are very infrequent, the operator may be relied on to do the detection and the recovery.

If checking is being done at every resource request, then it becomes necessary, before halting process P for resource R, to check that this does not lead to a circular wait condition. A simple recursive algorithm will check this, as follows:

PROCEDURE check deadlock (p: process, r: resource)

    FOR all resources r' held by p DO
    FOR all processes p' halted for r' DO
      IF p' holds r THEN there is a deadlock
               ELSE check deadlock (p', r)

If checking is being done only periodically, then it is necessary to repeat this check for *all* resources. Note that the algorithm can be coded far more efficiently by tagging processes once they have been checked, so that there is no need to check them again.

Once a deadlock has occurred, an attempt must be made to recover the situation. This is likely to be quite drastic, involving abortion of at least one of the deadlocked processes, or preempting resources. Whether or not this is a satisfactory way of dealing with deadlocks depends on the frequency with which they arise and the cost and acceptability of the recovery measures. In some cases an occasional job lost (or restarted from the beginning) may be perfectly acceptable as long as it does not happen too often. In other cases it might be disastrous.

13.2.3 Deadlock avoidance

The avoidance technique involves dynamically deciding whether allocating a resource will lead to a deadlock situation. There are two common strategies that can be employed:

(1) Do not start a process if its demands might force a deadlock situation.

(2) Habermann's Algorithm (Habermann, 1969), also known as the 'Banker's Algorithm'.

Before considering the operation of these algorithms, suitable notation must be defined.

Consider a system running n processes, and with m different types of resources. Let

Vector $\mathbf{a} = \begin{pmatrix} a_1 \\ \cdot \\ \cdot \\ \cdot \\ a_m \end{pmatrix}$ gives the total amount of each resource in the system

$$
\text{Matrix B} = \begin{pmatrix} b_{11} & \cdots & b_{n1} \\ \cdot & & \cdot \\ \cdot & & \cdot \\ \cdot & & \cdot \\ b_{1m} & \cdots & b_{nm} \end{pmatrix} = (b_1, \; b_2, \; b_3, \; \cdots \; b_n)
$$

gives the requirements of each process for each resource. That is, b_{ij} = maximum requirement of process i for resource j (assuming that this information is known when the process is started).

$$
\text{Matrix C} = \begin{pmatrix} c_{11} & \cdots & b_{n1} \\ \cdot & & \cdot \\ \cdot & & \cdot \\ \cdot & & \cdot \\ c_{1m} & \cdots & c_{nm} \end{pmatrix} = (c_1, \; c_2, \; c_3, \; \cdots \; c_n)
$$

gives the current allocations. That is, c_{ij} = amount of each resource j allocated to process i.

Obviously:

(1)   For all k, $b_k \leqslant a$ (no process can claim more resources than the total available)

(2)   For all k, $c_k \leqslant b_k$ (no process is allocated more than its total maximum requirement)

(3) $\displaystyle\sum_{k=1}^{n} c_k \leqslant a$ (at most all resources are allocated)

One possible strategy, which cannot deadlock, is to start a new process P_{n+1} only if

$$
a \; \geqslant \; \sum_{k=1}^{n} b_k \; + \; b_{n+1}
$$

That is, process P_{n+1} is started only if its requirements can be fully satisfied should all processes claim their maximum requirements. This strategy is less than optimal as it assumes that all processes will make their maximum demand together. In general they will not do so, and

$$
c_k \; \ll \; b_k
$$

13.2.4 The Bankers Algorithm

In order to implement this allocation algorithm correctly, it requires that:

(1) The maximum resource requirement of each process is stated in advance (for example, when the process is created).

(2) The processes under consideration are independent (that is, the order in which they execute is immaterial; there are no synchronisation constraints).

(3) There are no real-time constraints; that is, it must be acceptable for a process to be held up for long periods whenever it makes a resource request. (In systems of cooperating processes, this can be relaxed if it is known that all processes hold resources for only a short time.)

Provided that these conditions are satisfied, the following resource allocation strategy (process P requesting resource R) can be applied.

(1) Use the Banker's Algorithm to determine whether allocating R to P will result in an unsafe state.

(2) If so, halt P; otherwise, allocate R to P.

A safe state is one in which there is at least one order in which the processes can be run which does not result in a deadlock. Let such a sequence be

$$S = P_{s1}, \ P_{s2}, \ \dots \ P_{sn}$$

That is, P_{s1} is run, then P_{s2} ... The state must be safe if even in the worst case (all processes request their maximum allocations) deadlock will not occur.

For this to be true:

$$\text{resources available } (a - \sum_{k=1}^{n} c_k) \geqslant b_{s1} - c_{s1}$$

to allow P_{s1} to run.

After P_{s1} has run its resources c_{s1} will be freed, so for P_{s2}

$$a - \sum_{k=1}^{n} c_k + c_{s1} \geqslant b_{s2} - c_{s2} \quad \text{etc.}$$

In general, a sequence S must exist such that for all processes P_k, the total resources minus the resources currently allocated to all processes after P_k in the sequence must be $\leqslant b_k$ (= maximum requirement for P_k). A resource request can be granted without the danger of deadlocks only if the resultant state is safe, otherwise the requesting process must be halted until more resources become available.

Having established that a safe sequence exists, it is not necessary deliberately to run processes in that sequence – once a deadlock situation is approached, a safe sequence will be enforced as a result of more processes becoming halted.

To prove that a state is safe, a sequence must be found that satisfies the resource allocation conditions specified above. However, there are n! possible sequences, and it would be impractical to try them all. Fortunately, if several processes can be run first, then as far as this algorithm is concerned, it does not matter which is actually chosen first. This means that a safe sequence can be determined as follows:

(1) Find any P_k that can be completed.

(2) Assume P_k is completed and release its resources.

(3) If any more processes are left – repeat from (1).

If at stage (1) no process P_k can be completed, that state is unsafe.

In some cases this solution to the deadlock problem is not completely satisfactory. The insistence of the Banker's Algorithm on independent processes may be unrealistic. Furthermore, in many cases, a near-deadlock can be almost as undesirable as a deadlock, as it forces the system to stop multiprogramming and may drastically affect performance. Thus there are other practical measures that may be applied as well as, or in some cases, instead of those given above. These are mainly of a 'tuning' nature and involve adjustment of parameters to ensure that deadlocks are extremely unlikely to arise. For example, a system may stop accepting jobs when the amount of free backing store is low, or cease scheduling certain classes of jobs when resources are heavily utilised.

13.3 REFERENCES

P. Brinch Hansen (1977). *The Architecture of Concurrent Programs*, Prentice-Hall, Englewood Cliffs, N.J..

E. G. Coffman, M. Elphick and A. Shoshani (1971). 'System Deadlocks', *Computing Surveys*, Vol. 3, pp. 67–78.

A. N. Habermann (1969). 'Prevention of System Deadlocks', *Communications of the ACM*, Vol. 12, pp. 373–385.

A. N. Habermann (1978). 'System Deadlocks', *Current Trends in Programming Methodology*, Vol. III, Prentice-Hall, Englewood Cliffs, N.J., pp. 256–297.

C. A. R. Hoare (1978). 'Communicating Sequential Processes'. *Communications of the ACM,* Vol. 21, pp. 666–667.

13.4 PROBLEMS

1. Describe how deadlocks can occur in multiprogramming systems and discuss scheduling strategies that aim to avoid them.

2. Define the term 'deadlock'.

3. Give an example of deadlock that involves only a single process and also an example involving two processes.

4. What is a deadlock situation in a multiprogramming system and what are the criteria for it to occur? Describe the three general techniques for solving the deadlock problem, and explain Habermann's algorithm.

5. Describe the possible different philosophies to overcome the problems of deadlock.

6. Why is recovery from a deadlock situation a difficult problem?

14 Resource Management – Protection

14.1 INTRODUCTION TO PROTECTION SYSTEMS

In chapter 13 one of the major problems of resource allocation, that of processes deadlocking, was considered. In this chapter the second major problem will be considered, that of control of access to the resources – that is, controlling *who* can perform *which operations* and on *which objects*.

Protection systems have mainly evolved in connection with areas or segments of store, with other resources being managed in more or less ad hoc ways. However, some of the more general protection systems are suitable for managing all of the resources of a computer system. The requirement for protection arose initially in order to protect the operating system against its users – that is, to prevent a user job from overwriting its code and data, and from taking control of its devices. Thus the emphasis in protection systems was on restricting the operations that a user could perform. Earlier chapters on store management showed how this could be implemented using base-limit registers or similar paging hardware. Most of the protection systems in use today reflect this, in that they recognise two distinct 'execution states', *user* and *supervisor* (different systems use different terms for the two states). In supervisor state, everything is permitted; in user state, some restrictions are enforced.

With the development of multiprogramming systems, there arose also a need to protect independent user computations from one another. However, the two-state systems developed for protecting the operating system were sufficient for this. In principle, a privileged operating system is able to implement any required degree of interuser protection. Thus, for example, quite complex mechanisms can be devised and implemented to allow users to share one anothers' files in a controlled manner.

The problem with this philosophy is that, as operating systems increase in size and complexity, it has become quite likely that the operating system itself will contain errors. If the whole of the operating system was privileged, then an error in any part of it could cause trouble. This led to the desire to protect *parts* of the operating system from other parts, and so more complex protection systems recognising more than two states were developed. The first major system to incorporate many protection states was MULTICS. In MULTICS the protection states were ordered into a hierarchy, from most privileged to least privileged, the idea being that only a small part of the operating system would run in the most privileged levels.

The last major development in protection resulted from a desire to produce more symmetrical protection systems. Up to this point, protection tended to work in a hierarchical fashion, so that A might be protected from B, but then B was not protected from A. This sufficed for protection within the operating system, though many people observed that the modular structure of an operating system did not really give rise to a hierarchy of privilege. However, as the use of computers increased, cooperation between users in the form of sharing programs and files became more common and in this context it became highly desirable to allow two programs to cooperate even when neither one trusted the other. This led to the development of the non-hierarchical protection system that permitted the safe cooperation of mutually suspicious programs.

14.2 A GENERAL MODEL OF PROTECTION SYSTEMS

A protection system manages the control of access to resources. More specifically, it is concerned with two kinds of entity:

> (1) *Objects* - the resources to be protected. Associated with each object is a *type* (for example, process, file, lineprinter, etc.) which determines the set of *operations* that may be performed on it (for example, start, kill, read, delete, print, etc.).

> (2) *Subjects* - the individuals wishing to access (that is, perform operations on) objects. Depending on the system, subjects may be users, processes, procedures, etc.

The function of a protection system is to define and enforce a set of access rules, just as encountered with segment and file accesses. The access rules may be regarded as relations between subjects and objects: associated with each (subject, object) pair is an *access right* which defines the set of operations that this particular subject may perform on this particular object. Obviously an access right may specify a subset of the total set of operations defined on an object, as determined by its type. Normally we shall be interested in subjects that are *processes*. The set of objects that a process can access at any given time is referred to as its *domain*. In describing a particular system, the following must be defined:

(1) How the domain of a process is represented in the protection system and how the protection rules are actually enforced.

(2) Under what circumstances, and in what ways, can a process move from one domain to another – that is, can it gain and lose access rights as a result of executing certain types of operation?

14.2.1 Defining and representing domains

There are many ways in which the access rules may be represented and these give rise to different kinds of protection systems. Perhaps the most obvious representation is in the form of an *access matrix* that hold the rights for each (subject, object) pair.

	Object A	Object B
Subject 1	Read Write	
Subject 2	Read	Read Write

Figure 14.1 Domain access matrix

For example, the situation shown in figure 14.1 would allow subject 1 to perform READ and WRITE operations on object A, and no operations at all on object B; subject 2 has READ permission for object A, and READ and WRITE permission for object B. In practice, the rights would probably be encoded as bit patterns, but even so, the access matrix would most likely be both large and sparse and so alternative methods of representation are normally used.

The most common sparse matrix representations are to store the matrix separately by row and by column, and these form two common protection systems. Storing by row gives, for each subject, a list of the rights of that subject to the various objects. The above access matrix:

        SUBJECT 1:   OBJECT A(READ, WRITE)
        SUBJECT 2:   OBJECT A(READ); OBJECT B(READ, WRITE)

Rights expressed in this form are called *capabilities*. A protection system based on capabilities gives each subject a list of capabilities, one for each object it may access, and requires that the appropriate capability be presented to the subject each time that an object is accessed. The capability is regarded as a 'ticket of authorisation' to access; ownership of a capability implies the right to access. How this works will be explained later. As a simple example, the segment table in a segmented system is in effect a capability list and each entry is a capability. However, the term 'capability system' is usually reserved for systems that take advantage of the capability structure to provide a general means for defining and changing domains within a process.

Storing the access matrix by columns, a list of the subjects that may access each object is obtained. Using the same example:

OBJECT A: SUBJECT 1 (READ, WRITE); SUBJECT 2 (READ)
OBJECT B: SUBJECT 2 (READ, WRITE)

This representation is called an *access list*, and is quite commonly used in file directories.

Capability lists and access lists are, in a sense, the two 'pure' representations of the protection rules. Each has its own particular advantages. Capabilities allow rigid checking of access rights, as the appropriate rights are presented by the subject on each access, but make it rather difficult for the owner of an object to revoke or change the rights given to others (as the capabilities are stored with the subjects rather than the objects). Access lists tend to give slower checking as a search is required to find the appropriate right, but do allow much easier alteration of rights. Consequently, some systems use a combined technique. For example, a file directory may contain access lists, which are checked only on opening a file. If the file is successfully opened, a capability for it is generated and used in all further accesses by this job. Since this kind of capability lasts only for the duration of a job, there is no difficulty in deleting or changing rights.

There is a third method of representing protection information. This is referred to as a 'lock-and-key' system and is quite commonly used because it leads to an extremely efficient access authorisation procedure. It involves associating a 'lock' (effectively, a sort of password) with each object and giving a 'key' to each subject authorised to use the object. The key must be presented on every access to the object, and the access is allowed only if the key matches the lock. Unlike a capability, the key does not identify a particular resource uniquely; several resources tend to be grouped together and given the same key, because locks and keys are usually restricted in size to obtain an efficient hardware implementation. Thus lock-and-key systems tend to be rather less general but potentially more efficient than the other two methods.

An example of a lock-and-key system is the MULTICS hierarchical protection system. This deals with the access rights of processes (subjects) to segments (objects). All the segments accessible to a process are described by entries in its segment table which thus acts as a kind of capability list. However, associated with each segment (in its segment table entry) is a 4-bit lock. The 4-bit key is held in the processor status register and defines the currently active domain. Access to the segment is permitted provided that the value of the key is not greater than the value of the lock.

Thus, *within each process* there is a hierarchy of sixteen domains corresponding to the sixteen possible key values. With key zero, everything can be accessed. With key 1, everything except segments with lock = 0 can be accessed, and so on. This is a generalisation of the two-level protection schemes commonly employed on conventional systems.

It should be noted that the precise definition of a 'matching' key in a lock-and-key system determines the number of domains and the relations between them. For example, with a 4-bit lock-and-key system any of the following could be used:

(1) Key ≤ Lock. This gives sixteen hierarchically ordered domains such that the access rights of domain i are a subset of those of domains 0 ... i - 1.

(2) Key = Lock. This gives sixteen non-overlapping domains - that is, there are no common resources between the domains.

(3) (Lock AND Key) ◇ 0. That is, some bits set in both lock and key. This again gives sixteen domains, but with only a partial ordering between domains, so that some domains are disjointed while others overlap with one another.

14.3 INTERDOMAIN TRANSITIONS

So far several different ways in which protection domains can be defined and represented in a computer system have been described. However, it is also necessary to identify exactly how a process can transfer between different domains in the course of execution. The 'ideal' would be to enable the process at any instant to have access only to those objects that it needs in order to perform its current task. This implies a very high rate of switching between domains, say on every procedure call.

Protection systems can be loosely classified into three types according to how domain changes are achieved. In the simplest type of system, a process cannot switch between domains and the access rights change only on switching to another process. The most general type of system permits arbitrary changes between domains on each procedure call, allowing the 'ideal' mentioned above to be achieved. Such systems are usually based on capabilities, as these are the only representation that can efficiently support such a general system. The third kind of system allows changes of domain on procedure calling, but restricts the kind of domain change allowed. These are usually based on lock-and-key representation systems and the restrictions depend on the particular choice of lock and key. Restricted systems are attractive in spite of the fact that they cannot achieve the 'ideal', because they can at least be built at a reasonable cost.

The three types of system are discussed in more detail below.

14.3.1 Domain changes only on process changes

This is a static kind of protection system that can be implemented with simple two-state (user/supervisor) machines as it requires only a means of separating processes from one another. On the whole it is quite adequate for protecting user jobs from one another, but tends to lead to a large and privileged operating system.

If it is required to protect parts of the operating system from one another, then it is necessary effectively to run each module as though it were a separate user job. Then, only a small part of the system (a kernel, responsible for dealing with protecting and multiprogramming user jobs) needs to be privileged. However, the other modules (most user jobs) need a means of communicating with one another and so a message system must be provided by the kernel to allow this. Processes (modules) then communicate by passing messages to one another. This, in theory, can give a completely safe and general protection system by isolating each small operating system function within its own protected 'virtual machine'. However, the message and process changing costs can be high if the partitioning into virtual machines is taken too far!

The Manchester MUSS operating system (Frank and Theaker, 1979) is based on this protection philosophy, as it allows a quite general, portable system to be constructed using conventional hardware.

14.3.2 Restricted domain change systems

In this class of system, each process has a restricted set of domains associated with it (as determined by the key values of a lock-and-key domain system) and a controlled means is provided for switching between domains on certain procedure calls. While not completely general, they do permit some distinction in the accessing of rights for different parts of a process. As a practical example of this kind of system, the MULTICS hierarchical protection system (Schroeder and Salzer, 1972) will be considered in some detail. Similar systems have been implemented on other machines such as the ICL 2900.

As mentioned previously, MULTICS uses a lock-and-key representation for domains. The system is primarily concerned with controlling access to segments and so the lock is a 4-bit number held in the segment table entry for each segment. The 4-bit key is held in the processor status register and defines the currently active domain. Access is permitted to a segment provided that the current key value is not greater than the lock for the segment; further access bits then determine the kind of accesses that can be made (for example Read, Write and Execute). So, the access check procedure on each access to the store can be described as:

    IF pstatus. key ≤ segtable[s]. lock
        AND requiredoperation ≤ segtable[s]. accessrights
        THEN (access to segment s is permitted)

This enables each process to have sixteen domains, corresponding to the sixteen different key values, and to arrange the domains in a hierarchy from most privileged (key = 0) to least privileged (key = 15).

Clearly, for the protection system to operate, the user must be restricted from accessing the processor status register. If the user could write arbitrary values into the KEY field of this register, then the protection system is completely useless. In fact, the KEY field can be changed only indirectly as a result of calling a procedure in a different segment, and hence possibly in a different domain. When this is done, the hardware first checks that the call is legal (that is, it satisfies the protection rules) and then changes the key value if necessary.

Procedure calling is controlled by an extra access control bit, in addition to the normal READ, WRITE and EXECUTE permissions, that defines a permission to 'CALL' a procedure within a segment. The hardware action on calling a new procedure p in a new segment s is:

    IF pstatus. key ≤ segtable[s]. lock
        AND call ≤ segtable[s]. accessrights
        AND p is a valid entry point to the segment
            THEN pstatus. key : = segtable[s]. newkey
                segtable[s]. rights : = segtable[s]. rights + execute

Note that three separate checks are required:

(1) that the present domain can access the segment at all
    (pstatus. key ≤ segtable[s]. lock).

(2) that it has permission to CALL procedures in the segment
    (call ≤ segtable[s]. accessrights).

(3) that the point to be entered is a valid procedure entry point (one

possible check that could be used is that the entry point is in the first n words of the segment).

The last check is important, as arbitrary damage can be caused if a privileged procedure is entered at some undefined point rather than at its start.

In the course of entering the procedure, the hardware must also set the KEY to the appropriate value for the called procedure (from the segment table), and set Execute permission in the rights for the segment to allow code to be executed in the segment subsequently. (Thus, even if the segment did not originally have to execute permission, provided that it is CALLed at a valid point it can be executed.)

The main problems with this kind of organisation are:

(1) Validation of reference parameters - when a procedure A is calling a procedure B, it is possible to pass a pointer that is accessible to B but not to A. Strictly, such a call should be made illegal.

(2) Call to less privileged procedures (for example, procedures supplied as parameters to privileged procedures). Here, the less privileged procedure cannot be given access to the caller's stack and so a new stack in a new segment must be created for the duration of the call. This in turn complicates parameter passing.

(3) The restriction of domains being a hierarchy mean that general problems, such as the cooperation of mutually suspicious procedures, cannot be solved.

14.3.3 Arbitrary domain changes

Systems permitting arbitrary changes of domain are generally implemented using capabilities, since lock-and-key systems cannot support arbitrary domains and access control lists are slow in use. For an efficient system, hardware implementation of capabilities is essential.

A capability is a ticket authorising its holder to access some object. In general, a capability needs to give three items of information about the object:

(1) The TYPE of the object - for example, SEGMENT, PRINTER, FILE, etc. The type of an object defines which operations make sense on it.

(2) The IDENTIFICATION of a particular object.

(3) The ACCESS RIGHTS to the object – that is, the subset of the operations defined for this particular object type that the capability authorises the holder to perform.

To prevent the user from generating arbitrary capabilities, which would obviously totally invalidate the protection system, capabilities are normally held together in a capability segment. This is like a normal segment except that it does not have the usual read, write or execute permissions. Instead, it has the access permissions READ CAPABILITY and WRITE CAPABILITY, allowing the process to use its contents as capabilities (but not data) and to store capabilities (but not data) into it. The current 'domain' will be defined by such a capability segment: any objects for which the current capability segment contains a capability can be accessed but other objects cannot. Thus, changing from one domain to another involves altering the hardware register that points to the current capability segment (in this context, 'points' actually means 'contains a capability for').

As always, of course, changes of domain need to be carefully controlled as a process cannot be allowed to change its domain without somehow checking that the change is a valid one. As with the MULTICS system, this checking is achieved by binding domain changes to the procedure call operation so that a change of domain can occur only on switching to a new procedure. Again, a new type of access right, CALL, is introduced to control the operation of calling a 'protected' procedure (that is, one requiring a domain change). Corresponding to this is a hardware procedure call instruction, which has as its operand (a capability describing) a new capability segment. The call procedure operation can be defined as:

call procedure (s)

```
    IF s.type = segment
    AND call ≤ s.accessrights
        THEN currentdomain := s
                set readcapability and writecapability permission
                    into currentdomain.accessrights
                set currentproceduresegment := first capability
                    in segment s (effectively, a jump)
```

The following points are worth noting as compared with the MULTICS system. Firstly, the need explicitly to check whether the current domain is permitted to access the procedure specified is no longer necessary. The fact that the current domain can produce a capability for the procedure means that it must be allowed to access the procedure. There is, however, an extra type checking operation if capabilities are used to describe resources other than segments. Also, there is no longer the need to index into a segment table to check the access rights – they are already there in the capability presented (which presumably has already been taken out of the caller's capability segment, in effect a segment table). The domain change operation involves setting the hardware 'current capability segment' register and augmenting its access rights to include READ and WRITE CAPABILITY, and then entering the procedure. Once again, if it were required to pack more than one procedure into a segment, then a 'valid entry point' check would be needed, as in the MULTICS system.

In the relatively simple system described above, a total change of domain occurs on entering a protected procedure. No objects are common to the two domains unless they are explicitly placed in the called domain prior to the call, and allowing this would be dangerous. In a practical system, therefore, the current domain is represented by several capability segments, not just one. The Cambridge CAP computer recognises four distinct components of the current domain:

(1) Global data, which is not changed at all on a protected procedure call — that is, it is common to all domains.

(2) Local data, which is created afresh within the called procedure on each activation.

(3) Own data, which 'belongs' to the procedure and retains its values even when the procedure is not active. This is changed on every protected procedure call in the manner described above.

(4) Parametric data, which is passed from the caller to the called procedure.

Thus the current domain is represented by four capabilities, two of which are changed on a protected procedure call [(3) and (4)].

14.4 AN EXAMPLE OF A CAPABILITY SYSTEM

Capability systems can provide the mechanism whereby processes can switch between a set of arbitrary domains in a completely controlled manner. Using them, it is possible to implement the 'ideal' of giving a process access only to those objects that it needs to perform its current task. However, such systems introduce new problems — for example, how are protected procedures actually created? Ideally users would be able to create them but obviously there must be some control over this. A system called HYDRA will now be considered; developed at Carnegie-Mellon University, it illustrates how some of these problems can be solved.

Consider a file system in which files are protected by capabilities. The operations on files implemented by this basic file system might be:

READ BLOCK, which reads a specified block of the file
WRITE BLOCK, which writes a specified block to the file
DELETE, which deletes the file

Now suppose that a new kind of file is to be created using the above basic file system. This new file is a SEQFILE or sequential file, to which the following operations apply:

READ NEXT CHARACTER
WRITE NEXT CHARACTER
APPEND CHARACTER (adds a character to the end of the file)
DELETE

With such a set of operations, files could be created that can only be read character by character, or that can only be added to at the end.

A capability for a SEQFILE will have TYPE = 'SEQFILE', and the access rights will be some subset of those given above. However, the actual object itself will be a file in the basic file system and the only operations that are permitted on it are READBLOCK, WRITEBLOCK and DELETE. The procedure that implements the READ CHARACTER operation will need to be able to change the capability so that its type is 'FILE' and its access rights include READ BLOCK. This is known as an access amplification and is obviously a highly dangerous operation that must be carefully controlled. Before it can be discussed further, the concept of type as it applies to a protection system must be considered in more detail.

14.4.1 Types and access amplification

It has already been said that the type of an object defines the set of operations that can be peformed on it. For a static system, in which 'user' and 'system' are well-defined terms, this is sufficient. The user asks to perform an operation, the system interprets the access rights to check if the operation is allowed and, if so, performs the operation.

A problem arises when the idea of the 'system' as a static, monolithic entity is dropped. In the above example, an attempt was made to extend the system in such a way that

(1) the extensions were themselves fully protected – that is, they would be as secure as the rest of the system – but

(2) the extensions did not in any way compromise the security of the existing system. That is, even if the SEQFILE implementation was incorrect it could not possibly break any of the protection rules relating to the existing object type FILE.

This kind of extension is obviously essential if arbitrarily complex systems are to be built in a systematic way such that additions cannot wreck the operation of parts that already work.

Once the idea of building a system as a sort of hierarchy of subsystems, as above, is accepted, a more carefully defined concept of type is needed. The type of an object must now define both

(1) what the object actually consists of - that is, how it is implemented - and

(2) what operations can be performed on it.

If a new type of object is defined, saying what it consists of and what operations are valid on it, then procedures can be written to perform these operations. It is here that both access checking and access amplification are required. Checking is needed to ensure that the operation about to be performed is actually allowed, and amplification has to obtain for the operation-defining procedure the rights that it needs to perform the operation.

Amplification is achieved by an operation AMPLIFY with two parameters. The first is the capability to be altered and the second is a capability for a special kind of object called an amplification template. The template is the means of controlling access amplification, and gives:

(1) The TYPE of object whose access is to be amplified.

(2) The rights that must be present in order for the amplification to work.

(3) The new type that is to be set after amplification.

(4) The new set of rights to be set after amplification.

The operation can then be defined as:

amplify (c, t)

```
IF c. type = t. type
   AND t. rights ≤ c. rights
        THEN c. type := t. newtype
             c. rights := t. newrights
```

Thus, by calling 'amplify', a procedure will check the access permission on the parameter it has been given and perform the amplification required, provided that it has the suitable template available. For example, the template needed for the READ NEXT CHARACTER operation would be:

```
type = seqfile
rights = readnextcharacter
newtype = file
newrights = readblock
```

Normally, only the creator of a type would be allowed to create templates for that type, and so the entire mechanism is secure. This control is, of course, also achieved by using capabilities, as outlined below.

14.4.2 Creation of new types

A standard system command NEWTYPE is used to create new object types. This is supplied with:

(a) the name of the type
(b) information about what the type consists of
(c) the names of operations that apply to the type

It returns a new capability for an object of type TYPE, and with access rights CREATE, DELETE, CHANGERIGHTS, TRANSFER and TEMPLATE. The capability is put away in the user's directory for future use.

The five access rights CREATE, DELETE, CHANGERIGHTS, TRANSFER and TEMPLATE refer to five standard operations defined by the system on objects of type TYPE. CREATE(T) creates a capability for a new object of type T (compare this with NEW in PASCAL). DELETE(T) deletes the type T. CHANGERIGHTS enables a capability to be constructed with access rights that are a subset of those in the given capability. Thus CHANGERIGHTS is not a protection hazard. TRANSFER can be used to give access to an object of type T to another user (that is, to place a capability for it in his directory). A combination of CHANGERIGHTS followed by TRANSFER can thus be used to give another user a capability with fewer rights than those of the donor. TEMPLATE is used to create an amplification template for an object of this type. Normally, the creator of a type will not give any other user a capability containing TEMPLATE rights and so only the creator will be able to create templates for the type. These will be embedded in the OWN data areas of the procedures performing operations on the type.

14.4.3 An example

Returning to original SEQFILE example, NEWTYPE can be used to create a new type of object called SEQFILE, which consists of a FILE with the operations READCH, WRITECH, APPENDCH defined in addition to the standard operations DELETE, CHANGERIGHTS and TRANSFER. This will give a new capability, with:

```
type = TYPE
identification = 'SEQFILE'
rights = (CREATE, DELETE, CHANGERIGHTS, TRANSFER, TEMPLATE)
```

The TEMPLATE rights can now be used to create amplification templates for the operations READCH, WRITECH, APPENDCH, and these can be used to implement the three operations.

CREATE rights can be used to create a new SEQFILE object, which can then be accessed using the operations READCH, WRITECH, APPENDCH and the standard operations including DELETE. Note that READBLOCK or WRITEBLOCK cannot be used directly unless we cheat and call AMPLIFY directly.

CHANGERIGHTS and TRANSFER can be used to give access to a SEQFILE to someone else. It can also be arranged that they have the same rights or a subset. Incidentally, since TRANSFER is automatically defined for all types, the ability of the recipient of a SEQFILE to pass it on to someone else can be controlled.

CHANGERIGHTS and TRANSFER can also be used to give someone else access to the *type* SEQFILE (as distinct from giving them individual SEQFILE objects), but usage of this *type* would then be rather obscure.

14.5 REFERENCES

G. R. Frank and C. J. Theaker (1979). 'The Design of the MUSS Operating System', *Software – Practice and Experience*, Vol. 9, pp. 599–620.

R. M. Graham (1968). 'Protection in an Information Processing Utility', *Communications of the ACM*, Vol. 11, pp. 365–369.

M. D. Schroeder and J. H. Salzer (1972). 'A Hardware Architecture for Implementing Protection Rings', *Communications of the ACM*, Vol. 15, pp. 157–170.

14.6 PROBLEMS

1. Discuss the need for the protection of resources.

2. How does a capability test differ from a simple access control test?

15 Process Synchronisation – Basic Principles

15.1 INTRODUCTION

Operating systems have so far tended to be regarded as a set of largely independent processes. After all, the tasks that are being performed are clearly defined and largely self-contained. In theory, many of these processes could be run in parallel, and if a multiprocessor system were available, then a separate processor could be allocated for each of them. In a single processor system, the processes have to be multiprogrammed, switching from one process to another according to a suitable scheduling algorithm.

In practice, the processes that constitute an operating system cannot be totally independent. For example, the input system has to inform the job scheduler of the location and identification of input documents. Therefore, there has to be a mechanism for *communication* between processes. The obvious solution to this is a shared data structure. In the example, this might be a list of jobs or documents, where entries are inserted by the input system and removed by the job scheduler. There are certain (obvious) rules that have to be obeyed with this type of communication:

(1) Information cannot be removed from a list until it has been placed there.
(2) Information placed in a list must not be overwritten with new information before it has been used.

In order to be able to conform to these rules, the processes may also need to share certain control variables, such as a job count. Accesses to both the shared variables and the main list are potentially very error prone, and faults in the communication between operating system processes will have a disastrous effect on the performance and reliability of the computer system. There are two main problem areas:

(1) process synchronisation
(2) process competition

It will be shown that dependent processes can be cooperating, competing or both.

15.1.1 Process synchronisation

Processes must be able to inform one another that they have completed a certain action. This is necessary to satisfy the requirements for a communication system, namely that information must not be overwritten before the old information has been consumed, and that no attempt should be made to remove information before it has been made available. For example, in the first case, the input spooler might test the variable jobcount against some suitable limit, using a sequence such as

IF jobcount = joblimit THEN wait for prod

The input spooler can do nothing more until it receives a prod from the job scheduler to say that space is now available in the job list. A similar test and prodding mechanism is also necessary to test for an empty joblist.

15.1.2 Process competition

Whenever there are two processes trying to access a shared variable, there is a danger that the variable will be updated wrongly owing to peculiarities in the timing of the store accesses. For example, consider the input spooler and job scheduler concurrently accessing jobcount, then the actions they might perform are:

Input Spooler   jobcount := jobcount + 1
Job Scheduler   jobcount := jobcount - 1

If these processes are running in separate processors, which by chance try to execute these operations simultaneously, depending on which one completes last, the resulting values of jobcount will be either one too many or one too few. In the first case the system has apparently gained a job, whereas in the second case it has lost a job.

A similar effect can occur in a single processor system where processes are being multiprogramming. Consider a machine with a single accumulator (ACC), the actual machine instructions that are obeyed to perform these operations might be of the form:

```
ACC = jobcount              ACC = jobcount
ACC = ACC - 1      or       ACC = ACC + 1
ACC => jobcount             ACC => jobcount
```

Hence, process changing in the middle of these sequences can result in an incorrect value for jobcount, as shown below:

JOB SCHEDULER   INPUT SPOOLER

ACC = jobcount

An interrupt occurs (say) and the job scheduler is preempted to allow another process to process to service the interrupt. ACC is stored by the coordinator, to be restored the next time that the job scheduler is entered

                          The input spooler is entered and detects that the last peripheral transfer completed the input of a job
                          ACC = jobcount
                          ACC = ACC + 1
                          ACC => jobcount

Eventually the job scheduler is reentered and it resumes its execution with a new (incorrect) value in jobcount.
ACC = ACC - 1
ACC => jobcount

jobcount is now wrong!

From this example it can be seen that competition implies that processes are competing for some shared resource. The one basic rule in the case of competition is:

> only one process at a time should be allowed to access the shared resource

This is known as *mutual exclusion*. Apart from the synchronisation aspects, two of the other problems associated with mutual exclusion have already been encountered, namely:

(1) allocation – which processes are allowed to access the resource

(2) protection - how to prevent other processes from accessing the resource

These aspects were considered in chapters 13 and 14 on resource allocation. In this chapter the main concern is *how* to achieve mutual exclusion; that is, how to ensure that only one process at a time is doing a particular operation.

15.2 FLAGS

In order to deal in general with process competition, a means of making arbitrary sections of code mutually exclusive must be available. One way to achieve this in a multiprogramming system is to inhibit all interrupts during the execution of such code, but this is unsatisfactory since

(1) there is no direct equivalent for a multiprocessor system, and

(2) it reduces the ability of the system to respond rapidly to critical events.

The alternative approach is to precede all critical operations by a sequence of code that warns all other processes that someone is already executing a critical sequence. The most immediately obvious technique is to use a flag, thus:

```
WHILE flag = 0 DO (nothing)
flag := 0

critical section...

flag := 1
```

The problem with this is that the first two statements *themselves* constitute a critical section and require mutual exclusion - otherwise two processes could simultaneously find the flag non-zero and enter their critical sections. There is a solution to the mutual exclusion problem using only ordinary test and assignment operations (Dijkstra, 1965), but it is quite complex and will not be considered here. Thus the conclusion must be that what is really needed is some operation designed specifically for synchronisation purposes - a synchronising primitive.

The problem with the solution above results from the separation of the two operations (a) testing the flag and (b) modifying it. Probably the simplest operation that gets around this problem is one that *reads and clears* a variable in a single store cycle - that is, so that no other process may access the variable inbetween. Many machines have an instruction in their order code specifically for this reason. The *Read and Mark* (or *Read and Clear* order) has the effect of reading a store location into an accumulator and setting the store value to zero. (This is comparatively easy to implement on stores that are destructively read.) A suitable sequence might therefore be:

WHILE read and clear (flag) = 0 DO (nothing)

critical section

flag := 1

Now, because of the indivisibility of the read and clear operation, it is certain that only one process at a time can enter the critical region. This solution, however, suffers from two related defects. Firstly, it employs the 'busy' form of waiting — that is, processes waiting to enter critical sections are actively looping while they test the flag. This wastes processor time in a multiprogramming system and store cycles in the shared store of a multiprocessor system. Secondly, it is possible by chance for some process always to find the flag zero and hence never to enter the critical section if there are many other processes also accessing the flag. Although this may be improbable, the aim should be to make such situations impossible.

To avoid busy waiting, two operations can be introduced:

(1)   block   which halts the current process
(2)   wakeup(p)   which frees process p

In a true multiprocessor system these might be hardware operations that actually halt the processor. In a multiprogramming system they would be implemented by the coordinator performing the transitions RUNNING -> HALTED and HALTED -> READY. Using these two operations, the next iteration would be:

WHILE read and clear (flag) = 0 DO block

critical section. . . .

flag := 1
wake(one of the blocked processes, if any)

Again, errors could occur in this. Firstly, the block operation almost certainly involves updating a shared list of blocked processes for use in the wakeup sequence. This updating is probably fairly complicated and requires mutual exclusion! Secondly, it is possible for the following sequence of events to occur:

Process 1   Process 2

read and clear (flag)
and find it zero, thus deciding to
block. In the meantime, process 2
which is executing its critical section
at the time, completes it.

                                             . . .
                                             finish critical section
                                             flag := 1
                                             no   processes   blocked,   so
                                             process 2 just continues without
                                             freeing anyone.

block

Process 1 can now never be freed,
as a process is only ever freed by
another   process   in   its   critical
section

15.3 SEMAPHORES

To overcome the problems of synchronisation and mutual exclusion, a
primitive, known as a semaphore, has evolved (Dijkstra, 1968a).

A semaphore (s) is an integer variable on which three operations
have been defined:

   (1) Initialisation to a non-negative value
       s := initial value

   (2) wait(s)   (or p(s))
       IF s $\diamond$ 0 THEN s := s - 1
               ELSE block process

   (3) signal(s)   (or v(s))
       IF queue empty THEN s := s + 1
               ELSE free process

(The p and v mnemonics correspond to the Dutch equivalent of wait and
signal.)

For the time being, assume that the wait and signal operations are
indivisible and that there is no question of two processes simultaneously
incrementing or decrementing a semaphore. Their implementation will be
discussed later.

From the definition of the operations, an important property of semaphores, called the *semaphore invariant* can be derived. This is true of all semaphores and can be used to make mathematically precise statements about process synchronisation.

From the definition, if s is a semaphore, then

value(s) =   initial value(s)
            + number of signals(s) − number of completed waits(s)

and it can easily be seen that value(s) can never be negative. Thus, abbreviated slightly:

$$iv(s) + ns(s) - nw(s) \geq 0$$

This is the semaphore invariant. The following two simple examples will illustrate its use for showing the correctness of synchronisation.

15.3.1 Mutual exclusion by semaphores

Given the correct implementation (in hardware or software) of semaphores, mutual exclusion can be achieved by using a semaphore s initialised to 1 and surrounding each critical region by:

                    wait(s)
                        critical region
                    signal(s)

It is clear that the number of processes in critical regions is equal to the number that have performed a wait(s) without executing the corresponding signal(s); that is, nw(s) − ns(s). From the semaphore invariant, it can immediately be seen that nw(s) − ns(s) ≤ iv(s), and since iv(s) = 1 this gives 'number of processes in critical sections ≤ 1' − the definition of mutual exclusion.

15.3.2 Process communication using semaphores

Now consider a set of processes communicating via a shared buffer of N locations (such as the job scheduler and input system in the simple system). Each process that places data into the buffer is called a *producer*; each process removing data is a *consumer*. Two rules can be defined which must be obeyed for satisfactory communication between the processes:

(1) Number of items placed in buffer and not removed must be ≥ 0
(2) Number of items placed in buffer and not removed must be ≤ N

The two types of process can therefore be implemented using two semaphores:

  p which indicates a free position in the buffer and is initialised to N
  c which indicates data available in the buffer and is initialised to 0

Producer   Consumer

REPEAT   REPEAT
    produce item;   wait(c);
    wait(p)   take item from buffer;
    place item in buffer;   signal(p);
    signal(c);   process item;
FOREVER   FOREVER

Looking at the structure of the solution, it is easy to see that

(1) Number of items in buffer $\geqslant$ ns(c) – nw(c) = –iv(c) = 0
(2) Number of items in buffer $\leqslant$ nw(p) – ns(p) = iv(p) = N

So the communication constraints are satisfied.

From these examples it can be seen that, in order to *protect* a critical section of code, matching waits and signals are placed around the section. When using semaphores to *communicate* between processes, the waits and signals are placed in opposite processes.

The semaphore is a fairly primitive operation and, although it has worked well for these two cases, it can be difficult to use in more complicated problems. Hence it is probably best regarded as a low-level facility, used to implement other more manageable synchronisation facilities.

15.4 IMPLEMENTATION OF SEMAPHORES

The wait and signal operations are performed by the coordinator as it has the task of scheduling processes in a multiprogramming system (or allocating processors in a multiprocessor system). Naturally, it must maintain a list with an entry for each semaphore, as shown in figure 15.1.

Processes are entered on to the queue when they are blocked during the wait operation, and are removed during the signal operation.

It is through use of the wait and signal procedures that the coordinator knows which processes require to run at any instant in time. The operation of the coordinator can be roughly described as:

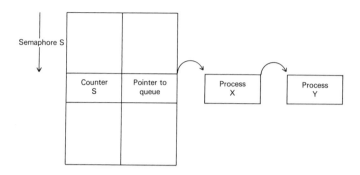

Figure 15.1 List of semaphores

```
REPEAT
    choose the highest priority free process;
    run it until either:
        (a) it halts (as a result of waiting on a zero-valued
            semaphore)
        (b) a higher priority process becomes free (as a result
            of a signal operation).
FOREVER
```

So far the following logical descriptions have been used as the
definitions of wait and signal:

wait(s):   IF s ◇ 0 THEN s := s − 1
              ELSE block process

signal(s):   IF queue empty THEN s := s + 1
              ELSE free process

A process attempting a WAIT operation on a zero-valued semaphore is
thus assumed to be held up until some other process performs a signal.
Explicit use has not been made of the value of the semaphore variable
(since no operation has been defined that allows this value to be
discovered). The only property used is the semaphore invariant:

$$iv(s) + ns(s) - nw(s) \geqslant 0$$

Any implementation must guarantee that this is always true. It is also
essential that the wait and signal operations should be indivisible in
order to ensure that it is impossible for (say) two processes
simultaneously to find the semaphore has a value of one and attempt to
decrement it. To achieve this, the operations must be implemented using

read and clear orders or by inhibiting interrupts. The precise technique depends on whether the operating system is running on a single or multiprocessor system. Each of these cases will now be considered.

15.5 SEMAPHORE IMPLEMENTATION FOR A MULTIPROCESSOR SYSTEM

In a true multiprocessor system there are two main approaches to implementing semaphores:

(1) Implement the wait and signal operations directly in hardware, achieving indivisibility by interlocks at the store interface (for example, by performing the entire operation in a single store cycle).

(2) Program the wait and signal operations, using a more basic hardware mechanism (for example, read and clear) to achieve the effect of indivisibility.

15.5.1 Hardware implementation

The fundamental hardware operations that correspond to wait and signal are, respectively:

(a) decrement and test
(b) increment and test

These may be combined with either a goto operation, or suitable blocking operations. For example

wait(s):   IF s := s − 1 < 0 THEN block

signal(s): IF s := s + 1 ≤ 0 THEN
                wakeup (one waiting processor)

could be implemented as single, elementary operations. Note that in this case the wakeup operation would pick a processor according to some fairly rigid hardware rule. For this reason semaphores are generally used without making any assumptions about which process will be freed by a signal. The ability to make such assumptions would considerably simplify the solutions of some problems where it is required to give some processes priority over others.

A second point to note is that in this implementation the actual value of the semaphore variable can become negative and, in this case, indicates the number of halted processes. Although it is specified that semaphores take only non-negative values, the synchronisation implied by this implementation is identical with that implied by the logical definition, since a process never passes a wait operation if the value of the semaphore is zero or negative. More formally, if the 'value' of the semaphore s is defined to be IF s $\geq$ 0 THEN s ELSE 0, it is easy to see that the semaphore invariant

$$value(s) = iv(s) + ns(s) - nw(s) \geq 0$$

still holds, and since this is the only property of semaphore that has been used, the synchronisation should still be correct.

15.5.2 Software Implementation

If the hardware does not perform the complete operation as above, then obviously some of it has to be programmed in software. This requires some means of ensuring mutual exclusion (that is, indivisibility) during the semaphore operations. If the read and clear operation is available in hardware, the following implementation will suffice:

```
wait(s):    WHILE read and clear(flag) = 0 DO (nothing)
            s := s - 1
            IF s < 0 THEN
               BEGIN
               add current process to s.queue
               block (must also set flag back nonzero)
               END
            ELSE flag := 1

signal(s):  WHILE read and clear(flag) = 0 DO (nothing)
            s := s + 1
            IF s ≤ 0 THEN
               BEGIN
               remove one process (p) from s.queue
               wakeup (p)
               END
            flag := 1
```

where s is the count used to represent the semaphore value, and s.queue is a queue of processes halted on the semaphore s. Note that if s < 0 then (-s) is the number of processes on s.queue.

The variable flag is used to guarantee mutual exclusion while accessing the semaphore. A separate flag could be used for each semaphore but it is unlikely that this would be worthwhile. Note also that the block operation must also release the mutual exclusion by setting flag non-zero.

'Busy waiting' is used in the case of accesses to flag, but not for halting on the semaphore itself. The flag is only held zero for a very short time and so busy waiting should not occur often or for long. Although it would be possible to replace the block with an equivalent 'busy wait', this would be unacceptable since processes there may halt for a considerable length of time.

In the absence of an operation such as read and clear, some other basic mutual exclusion mechanism, such as the one discussed by Dijkstra would have to be used.

15.6 SEMAPHORE IMPLEMENTATION FOR MULTIPROCESSING SYSTEMS

In a single-processor multiprogramming system, semaphore implementation can be simplified by inhibiting interrupts to obtain mutual exclusion. Thus all operations on flag in the above section are replaced as appropriate by the inhibiting and enabling of interrupts. Busy waiting is clearly unacceptable in this case as it would tie up the one and only available processor, preventing any other process from resetting the flag to 1. Block and wakeup are, of course, procedures implemented by the coordinator rather than hardware operations. They might therefore be implemented as follows:

```
wait (s)
                inhibit interrupts
                s := s - 1
                IF s < 0 THEN
                            add current process to queue s
                            block the process and allow interrupts
                ELSE
                            allow interrupts

signal (s)
                inhibit interrupts
                s := s + 1
                IF s ≤ 0 THEN
                            remove first process (p)
                            wakeup (p)
                allow interrupts
```

While it is not acceptable in general to achieve mutual exclusion by inhibiting interrupts, the semaphore operations could be regarded as an exception, particularly as they are comparatively short.

15.7 AN EXAMPLE IN THE USE OF SEMAPHORES - THE READERS AND WRITERS PROBLEM

Consider the problem in which:
  (1) Several concurrent processes wish to access a common file.
  (2) Some wish to read; some wish to write.
  (3) Shared read accesses to the file are required, but exclusive access is required for the writers.

The following two cases will be considered: (a) where readers have priority over writers, and (b) where writers have priority over readers.

This problem is fairly typical. For example, compare it with an airline reservation system where many enquiries on a central database are allowed, but only one travel agent/booking office at a time can be allowed to change the database and reserve a seat.

15.7.1 Readers have priority

Exclusive access to write to the file can be achieved with a single semaphore w.

Writing

```
            wait (w)

                exclusive access to
                alter the file.

            signal (w)
```

Reading

A variable readcount (initially 0) is needed to note how many processes are currently reading the file. The first reader sets the w semaphore to stop any writers, and the last reader clears the w semaphore.

```
wait (x)
     readcount := readcount + 1
     IF readcount = 1 THEN wait (w)
signal (x)

     read the file.

wait (x)
     readcount := readcount - 1
     IF readcount = 0 THEN signal (w)
signal (x)
```

Note that as the variable readcount is accessed by all readers concurrently, it must be 'protected' by including it in a critical region controlled by semaphore x.

As long as there is at least one process reading the file, any other readers can also access the file concurrently (although they must pass through the critical region protected by x one at a time).

If a process is writing to the file, the first reader will halt on semaphore w, and all other readers on semaphore x.

15.7.2 Writers have priority

In many respects the solution is the converse of the previous solution, in that:

(1) A semaphore r is needed to inhibit all readers while the writers are wanting to access the file.

(2) A variable writecount is needed to control the setting of r.

(3) A semaphore y is needed to control access to writecount.

(4) A semaphore w is still needed to achieve exclusive write access to the file.

Writing

	wait (y)
Stop	writecount := writecount + 1
Readers	IF writecount = 1 THEN wait (r)
	signal (y)

	wait (w)
Access the	write to the file
File	signal (w)

	wait (y)
Free	writecount := writecount – 1
Readers	IF writecount = 0 THEN signal (r)
	signal (y)

Reading

(1) Multiple reading must still be allowed, and so the variable readcount is still needed.

(2) The r semaphore must be set before the w semaphore is set. If w is set after, a deadlock situation could result.

(3) There must be a signal on the r semaphore before the reading sequence, as multiple reading is allowed.

(4) A long queue must not be allowed to build up on r, otherwise writers will not be able to jump the queue. Therefore only one reader is allowed to queue on r by waiting on an additional semaphore z immediately before the wait on r.

```
wait (z)
      wait (r)
            wait (x)
                  readcount : = readcount + 1
                  IF readcount = 1 THEN wait (w)
            signal (x)
      signal (r)
signal (z)

read the file

wait (x)
      readcount : = readcount - 1
      IF readcount = 0 THEN signal (w)
signal (x)
```

State of the queues

Readers only in the system	w set No queues
Writers only in the system	w and r set Writers queue on w
Both readers and writers with read first	w set by reader r set by writer All writers queue on w 1 reader queues on r Other readers queue on z
Both readers and writers with write first	w set by writer r set by writer Writers queue on w 1 reader queues on r Other readers queue on z

15.8 REFERENCES

E. W. Dijkstra (1968a). 'Cooperating Sequential Processes', *Programming Languages*, (ed. F. Genuys), Academic Press, New York.

E. W. Dijkstra (1968b). 'The Structure of the THE Multiprogramming System', *Communications of the ACM*, Vol. 11, pp. 341-6.

E. W. Dijkstra (1965). 'Solution of a Problem in Concurrent Programming Control', *Communications of the ACM*, Vol. 8, p. 569.

15.9 PROBLEMS

1. Explain why the semaphores WAIT and SIGNAL must be done indivisibly.

16 Process Synchronisation –
Advanced Techniques

16.1 INTRODUCTION

It has been shown how semaphores can be used for process
communication and to achieve mutual exclusion. They can, of course,
be used also for more complicated synchronisation problems. The main
advantage of semaphores over more ad hoc methods is that the
semaphore invariant provides a means of treating synchronisation
problems with mathematical rigour. It can actually be proved, rather than
just assumed that the solutions are correct.

The main problem with semaphores is that, for large and complex
systems, they leave considerable scope for programming errors, and it
is still quite easy to program systems containing time-dependent errors.
There has therefore been considerable research into alternative
techniques for constructing operating systems with reduced opportunities
for such errors. Two main approaches can be distinguished, which can
be characterised as (a) message based, and (b) language based.

The message based approach tries to provide operations more closely
suited to the needs of operating system modules than the primitive
semaphore operations. This makes the writing of the module more
simple, and tends to eliminate timing errors as synchronisation is
performed 'behind the scenes' by the higher-level operations. The
language based approach attempts to define programming language rules
which make it possible to detect potential time-dependencies by semantic
checks in the compiler. Thus, a program that compiles without errors
cannot exhibit any time-dependencies (though its synchronisation may
still not be correct!).

Examples of both these approaches will now be given, beginning with
the message-based one. It should be noted that many different forms of
each approach have been devised and it is not possible to consider all

of these.

16.2 MESSAGE SYSTEMS

Message systems were devised in an attempt to realise two important objectives in operating systems design. These are:

(1) Determinacy – the system's behaviour should not be timing-dependent. This has already been discussed at some length.

(2) Protection – because operating systems need to be altered frequently, and because these alterations may introduce errors, it is desirable to protect the individual modules of the system against the effects of errors in other modules so that an error in a relatively unimportant module does not crash the entire system.

The main problem with protecting modules from one another is that they need to share variables, and a fairly sophisticated protection system is required if they are to be allowed to share *only* certain variables. Furthermore, a module can quite easily destroy the operation of another by interfering with those variables that are shared.

The problem with determinacy, on the other hand, is that when synchronisation requirements become complex, their programming becomes quite difficult. It should be noted too that synchronisation arises *only* when processes share resources. If this sharing could be eliminated, then both the protection and the determinacy problems could be solved.

Processes that form part of an operating system cannot run in a vacuum – they have to communicate with one another. It is this need for communication that mainly results in processes sharing data. So, one approach in designing an operating system is to keep the processes separate – that is, not to allow them to share anything – and then provide them with an alternative means of communication by passing *messages* to one another.

If this approach is adopted, then operating system modules can be protected from one another using the same mechanisms that protect user jobs from one another (for example, base-limit registers). Clearly the message-passing module is an exception in that it is the only part of the system that needs explicitly to access shared data, and the only one that performs explicit synchronisation. Other modules synchronise indirectly via the message operations.

16.3 MESSAGE-PASSING OPERATIONS

Clearly the minimum set of operations needed are those to *send* and to *receive* messages. The receive operation will halt the process until a message is actually received; the send will free the destination process if it is waiting for a message.

Assuming a minimal system of this type, there are two ways in which it might be implemented. In the first the two processes are very closely synchronised. The destination process must be waiting for a message before the sender sends it (alternatively, the sender is halted if this is not so). This has the advantage of not requiring messages to be buffered but it implies an undesirable degree of synchronisation between communicating processes.

If processes are to be permitted to operate asynchronously, some form of buffering is required in the message system. If each process has associated with it a queue of messages not yet read (p.queue) and a semaphore controls this queue (p.sem), then the message operations can be implemented as:

send (message.dest)

wait (mbuf)	Wait for message buffer available
wait (mutex)	Mutual exclusion on message queue
acquire free buffer	
copy message to buffer	
link buffer to dest.queue	
signal (dest.sem)	Wake destination process
signal (mutex)	Release mutual exclusion

receive (message)

wait (own.sem)	Wait for a message to arrive
wait (mutex)	Mutual exclusion on message queue
unlink buffer from own.queue	
copy buffer to message	
add buffer to freelist	
signal (mbuf)	Indicate another message buffer freed
signal (mutex)	Release mutual exclusion

where mbuf is initialised to the total number of message buffers available, own and dest refer to the queue of messages for each process, and is initially zero.

There are three points worth noting about this system:

(1) Observe that it is vital to keep the two waits in the *send* and *receive* operations in the order specified. Reversing them could

lead to deadlocks.

(2) The solution above involves a deadlock danger if all message buffers are used up and no process can continue without first sending a message. This is especially serious if user jobs are allowed to use the message operations.

(3) Note the similarity between the above and the producer/consumer situation given earlier. Logically the two cases are the same.

16.4 PRACTICAL CONSIDERATIONS

While in principle the facilities described are sufficient for a message system, in practice there are some further considerations which tend to make actual systems more complex. Some of the most important of these are:

(1) Form of the message.
(2) Addressing of processes.
(3) Type of message queuing discipline.
(4) Message validation/protection.
(5) Message deadlocks.

Each of these will now be briefly discussed and the particular solutions adopted in the Manchester University MUSS operating system will be described.

16.4.1 Form of the message

This depends very much on the objectives of the message system. Some systems adopt the attitude that the message should be as small as possible, to minimise overheads – for example, a single word – and this is often implemented by a message passing command in hardware. If a large amount of data is to be passed, the data can be placed in a file and the message then contains the file name. This leads to significant overheads in the case where intermediate amounts of information are to be passed, which rather invalidates the reason for making the messages short in the first place.

MUSS is a partly message-based system. Certain key parts of the system communicate and synchronise directly, but the higher-level modules communicate via messages and are completely protected from one another. Here the approach adopted was (within reason) to allow messages to have arbitrary size. This is achieved efficiently by defining a message to be a segment of virtual store. It can then be passed efficiently by transferring a pointer from the sender's to the receiver's segment table.

Using this mechanism, complete input/output documents can be passed around the system efficiently as messages. For example, an input spooler simply reads characters into a segment (which looks like a large array!) and when a terminator is recognised, the whole segment is sent as a message to its destination.

In fact, a small amount of control information (about 100 bytes) is passed along with every message. This is used to indicate to the destination process what is to be done with the segment (for example, print it, file it). In cases where this short header is sufficient, the segment can be omitted entirely, and this option is often used for internal control messages and for interactive input/output.

16.4.2 Addressing of processes

Clearly it is necessary to have a way of specifying to the send message operation *which* process is to receive the message. This in itself presents no difficulties — each process can be assigned a unique name and this can be used for identification purposes. (There is, however, a problem of identifying processes in other machines in a multicomputer system.)

The main question that arises is: 'how do processes specify with whom they wish to communicate?'. In MUSS there are three possible techniques and these represent three different ways of using the message system.

(1) The destination process name is built in when the module is programmed. For example, processes communicating with the file manager will use a standard name for it.

(2) The destination process is specified at run time, say by users' job control statements. This applies to processes such as output spoolers; the user can select which device the output goes to by specifying the destination process name. Device controllers are given standard names such as LPT, PTP, etc.

(3) The message might be a reply to a process from which a message has just been received. For this purpose (but see also section 16.4.4 below) each message includes the identity of the sender to allow replies to be sent easily. This is useful for internal system messages (for example, 'Get me a file please' — 'Here it is') and also for interactive jobs, whose output is directed to the same terminal from which input was last received.

16.4.3 Type of message-queuing discipline

Obviously the simplest is a straightforward first-in-first-out queue, but this may not be satisfactory if some messages are more urgent than others. Alternatives may include specifying message priorities so that they can automatically be queued in some priority order, or allowing the destination process to inspect its message queue and select which message to read.

MUSS gives each process eight separate message queues (called channels) and the sender can choose to which channel a message is to be sent. The destination can then establish conventions as to the use of each channel, and may choose from which channel the next message is to be read. Thus, for example, an output spooler may reserve one channel for normal documents, one for high priority documents and one for operator requests, such as to abandon printing the current document or to start it again as the paper has torn.

16.4.4 Message validation/protection

A process may wish to restrict the set of processes from which messages will be accepted. One essential step to achieve this is for the system to supply, with each message, enough information about the sender (for example, process identifier, user identifier) for the receiver to validate the message. In addition to this, MUSS allows a process to set each of its message channels into one of three states:

> OPEN   – messages accepted from all sources
> CLOSED   – messages accepted from no sources
> DEDICATED   – messages accepted from a specified source

The message system automatically rejects messages that do not fall into an acceptable category. In addition, a process can specify that a channel is to be closed after one message has been accepted, thus protecting itself against a shower of messages being sent by some faulty process to which the channel is temporarily open.

16.4.5 Message deadlocks

Finally the question arises 'what if a process is waiting for a message which never comes?'. Of course, this means some part of the system is misbehaving, but one of the objectives is to enable each module to protect itself against errors in others. This is particularly important in a system like MUSS, where user jobs as well as system modules can send and receive messages. The solution adopted here is to specify a time limit when waiting for messages. If this is exceeded, the waiting process wakes up and is informed that no message exists. This is a useful mechanism, as it allows each process to effect some sensible recovery action if a process with which it is communicating fails to answer. It also has other uses – for example, timing out a job if the user fails to type anything for a long time.

16.5 SOLUTION OF THE READERS AND WRITERS PROBLEM USING MESSAGES

The easiest way of using a message system to solve the Readers and Writers problem is to have a process in control of the database, so that the other processes wishing to access the information in the files must send messages to the controlling process. In an ultra-secure system, the controlling process might be the only one allowed to access the file. The other processes then either request records from the controlling process or send records to be incorporated into the database. Although this is very secure and 'clean', as only one process ever accesses the files, it incurs a number of overheads, particularly as the controlling process is unable to service multiple read requests in parallel (as requested in the problem specification).

The most satisfactory solution is therefore for the controlling process to grant permission to access the file and to leave the actual file access to the individual processes. The sequences within the reading and writing processes might therefore be:

In reading process   *In writing process*

Send message asking for   Send message asking for
permission to read the file   permission to write to the file

Wait for a reply   Wait for a reply
to say 'ok'   to say 'ok'

READ THE FILE   WRITE TO THE FILE

Send message to say   Send message to say
'I have finished'   'I have finished'

No priority decisions are included within the reading and writing processes. All such decisions have to be made by the controlling process.

16.5.1 Design of the controlling process

The controlling process has to service three types of message, namely requests to read, requests to write and the 'I have finished' messages. It is far easier to organise the controlling process if these can be serviced independently, and so a separate channel might be dedicated for each type of message, namely:

        Channel 1 – Finished messages
        Channel 2 – Write requests
        Channel 3 – Read requests

The order of servicing the channels therefore has a bearing on the relative priorities of the Readers and Writers.

The algorithm in figure 16.1 is one possible way of organising the controlling process so that writers have priority (recall that this case was quite complex when implemented using semaphores). In addition to servicing write request messages before read request messages in order to achieve the necessary priority, a means of achieving mutual exclusion for the writers must be provided. This involves the use of a variable COUNT, which is initialised to 100 (assuming less than 100 readers at any one time). The action of the controlling process can therefore be summarised as:

IF count > 0   Service channels in the order
                      'I have finished'
                      Write requests
                      Read requests

IF count = 0   The only request outstanding is
                      a write request, so having told
                      the writer to proceed, wait for
                      an 'I have finished' message

IF count < 0   A writer has made a request but
                      is having to wait until the current
                      batch or readers have finished.
                      Therefore, service only the 'I have
                      finished' messages

When waiting for messages on a specific channel (say channel 1), it is quite probable that messages will be queued on the other channels. As the requesting processes are halted until they receive a reply to their messages, the message system provides an effective queuing mechanism for the halted processes.

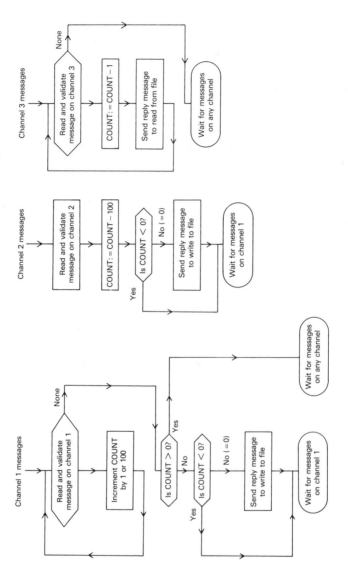

Figure 16.1 Control process for the readers and writers problem

16.6 THE LANGUAGE-BASED APPROACH - MONITORS

The language-based approach to operating system design aims to facilitate production of correct systems by defining the semantics of a programming language in such a way that the language cannot express timing-dependent errors of the kind that have been discussed. There have been many different attempts in this general direction. Probably the most successful was introduced by Brinch-Hansen, and subsequently developed by Hoare (Hoare, 1974) in the form of Monitors.

In monitors, two related concepts are combined, namely system modularity, and synchronisation. The form of modularity encouraged by monitors affords intermodule protection through static checks in the compiler. Thus, like message systems, monitors can be said to have both synchronisation and protection implications.

The approach taken to modularity is relevant to ordinary sequential programs as well as operating systems. The idea is that, when a structure is defined, the operations that can be performed on it should be defined at the same time, and the language semantics should prevent any other operations from being performed on it. As a simple (sequential) example, consider defining a stack data structure in Pascal. The definitions might be:

```
TYPE stack = RECORD
    st: ARRAY [1..maxstack] OF integer;
    sp: 1..maxstack
    END
```

The push and pop operations are then defined as:

```
PROCEDURE push (VAR s: stack; item: integer);
    BEGIN
    s.st[s.sp] := item;
    s.sp := s.sp + 1
    END;

PROCEDURE pop (VAR s: stack; VAR item: integer);
    BEGIN
    s.sp := s.sp - 1;
    item := s.st[s.sp]
    END
```

This is a perfectly good implementation of a stack but it leaves open the possibility to 'cheat' by accessing s.st or s.sp directly rather than via the push and pop procedures. For example, an instruction to throw away five items from the stack might be written as

$$s.sp := s.sp - 5$$

However, this precludes the ability to change the organisation of the stack, say to linked lists rather than arrays.

16.6.1 Encapsulation

A monitor encapsulates the definition of a data structure and the operations on it in such a way that the components of the structure can be accessed only from within the procedures that define operations on it. For example:

```
MONITOR stack;
    CONST maxstack = 100;
    VAR st: ARRAY [1..maxstack] OF integer
        sp: 1..maxstack;
    PROCEDURE push (item: integer);
        BEGIN
        st[sp] := item;
        sp := sp + 1
        END;
    PROCEDURE pop (VAR item: integer);
        BEGIN
        sp := sp - 1;
        item := st[sp]
        END;
    BEGIN
    sp := 1
    END;
```

This defines a new data type stack. So the variables can be declared in the usual way:

```
    VAR s1, s2: stack;
```

However, the components of S1 and S2 cannot be accessed; all that can be done is to call the push and pop procedures. The notation for doing this is similar to the notation for accessing components of record structures

```
    s1.push (item)
    s2.pop  (item)
```

Note that the monitor body defines the initialisation to be performed automatically on the data structures when it is declared.

For sequential programming the main advantage of this kind of structure lies in the enforcement of 'clean' programming techniques and the consequential improvement in maintainability of the software. Also, if program-proving techniques are ever to be useful, this kind of structuring seems essential – it enables a verification to be made that all uses of all stacks in a program are correct and only requires a check on about 20 lines of code.

16.6.2 Mutual exclusion

The first requirement with shared data structures is to provide mutual exclusion on accesses to them. With monitors this is easy. First the procedures of a monitor are mutually exclusive; that is, only one process at a time may be executing code within a given monitor. The compiler can implement this by associating a mutual exclusion semaphore with each monitor-type object declared. The semaphore is WAITED at the start and SIGNALLED at the end of each monitor call. An alternative for multiprogrammed systems that do not have fast crisis time devices is to inhibit interrupts throughout execution of monitor procedures.

Given this rule, and assuming that the language also has a means of defining processes, determinate operation can be guaranteed by the simple semantic rule: 'Processes may not share any data that is not accessed through a monitor'.

16.6.3 Communication

Mutual exclusion is only one part of the synchronisation problem. It is also necessary to provide the means whereby processes wait for something to happen, and are woken when it does. Many different mechanisms for this have been proposed, but two extremes are:

(1) High-level approach.
Since the waiting will be dependent on a shared data structure (for example, JOBCOUNT < 0), a statement

AWAIT <boolean expression>

can be introduced that can be used only within monitor procedures. The procedures delay the process until the boolean expression – which represents a relation on the monitor's data structure – is true. No explicit wake up operation is needed and any change to the data structure may implicitly wake a halted process.

(2) Low-level approach.
The alternative approach requires monitor procedures to synchronise explicitly using semaphores or a related mechanism. Obviously this will be rather less convenient but may be more efficient.

16.7 MODULA-2

Finally in this chapter, a language called MODULA-2 will be discussed. This language was designed in 1978 by Professor Niklaus Wirth, and is intended for the construction of system software on minicomputers. This language is based on Pascal, but has a number of interesting features that distinguish it from most other operating system languages. In particular:

(1) *MODULES*   As the name of the language implies, it is intended for the production of modular systems. To this end it includes a construct called a MODULE, which achieves the 'encapsulation' effect of monitors in a somewhat different way.

(2) *PROCESSES*   The language is designed primarily for writing multiprogramming systems for single-processor configurations. It therefore offers only very basic facilities for multiprogramming, which are firmly based on the concept of the coroutine. As a consequence, there is no built-in scheduling strategy; the system programmer is in full control.

(3) *DEVICES AND INTERRUPTS*   The language includes facilities for handling devices directly at the interrupt level. These are based on the PDP11 device driving and interrupt systems, but the principles could be extended to match other machines.

16.7.1 Modules

The module construct in MODULA-2 is designed to provide the 'escapsulation' of data and operations that were discussed in connection with monitors, but without the synchronisation implications. The form of a module declaration is:

```
MODULE module-name;
FROM other-module-name IMPORT identifier-list;
FROM yet-another-module-name IMPORT identifier-list;
. . .
EXPORT identifier-list;

block of code
```

Names from outside the module can be used only if they are mentioned in the IMPORT section, and the EXPORT section specifies names that can be used by other modules (provided that they IMPORT them). The notion of exports in MODULA-2 is more general than in monitors, as (a) the list of names to be exported is specified rather than exporting all procedure names, and (b) names other than those of procedures can be exported. This latter facility is particularly useful for exporting:

(1) Constants and read-only variables (though MODULA-2 does not include any way of specifying that an exported variable is read-only).

(2) Type identifiers, without necessarily exporting any information about the structure of the type.

It is recommended, but not mandatory, that shared variables (that is, variables shared between 'concurrent' activities) should be isolated within modules, which are then called interface modules.

16.7.2 Processes – coroutines

Coroutines are processes that are executed by a single processor one at a time. Transfers from one process to another are programmed explicitly.

MODULA-2 implements coroutines with a built-in type called PROCESS. This is in fact a structure used to keep the set of information, such as a register dump, needed to restart the process. However, the programmer is not able to access the contents of a PROCESS variable explicitly – the type PROCESS and the procedures that operate on variables of this type must be imported from a built-in module SYSTEM. A new process is initiated by declaring a variable of type process and then initialising it using the procedure NEWPROCESS

```
VAR p: process;

. . .

newprocess (code, base, size, p);
```

where code is the name of a procedure that specifies the actions of the new process, base and size are the address and size of the workspace to be used by this process and the variable p will subsequently be used to identify this process.

A transfer of control between two processes is then achieved by calling

```
transfer (p1,p2)
```

where p1 and p2 are both process variables. The effect is to:

(1) Suspend the current process and save its restart information in variable p1.

(2) Enter the process designated by p2.

16.7.3 An example module

As an example, the following is a simple process coordinator that implements a semaphore mechanism written in MODULA-2.

```
MODULE coordinator;
FROM SYSTEM IMPORT process, newprocess, transfer;
EXPORT sem, wait, signal, init;
CONST maxproc = 8;                        (number of processes)

TYPE sem = RECORD                         (semaphore data structure)
        c: 0..maxint;                     (semaphore count)
        q: 0..maxproc                     (queue header)
     END;

VAR proclist: ARRAY [1..maxproc] OF (process list)
        RECORD
        p: process;                       (process variable)
        s: (halted,free);                 (status)
        l: 0..maxproc                     (semaphore queue link)
     END;

     cproc: 1..maxproc;                   (current process)
     coord: process;                      (for return to coordinator)

PROCEDURE init (VAR s: sem; val: 0..maxint);
     (initialise semaphore)
     BEGIN
     s↑.c := val;                         (initialise count)
     s↑.q := 0                            (no processes halted)
     END;

PROCEDURE wait (VAR s: sem);
     BEGIN
     IF s↑.c > 0 THEN
        s↑.c := s↑.c - 1
     ELSE
        proclist[cproc].l := s↑.q;
        s↑.q := cproc;                    (add cproc to sem queue)
        proclist[cproc].s := halted;(mark cproc halted)
        transfer (proclist[cproc].p,coord)
     END
     END;
```

```
PROCEDURE signal (VAR s: sem);
    BEGIN
    IF s↑.q = 0 THEN                (no processes halted)
        s↑.c := s↑.c + 1
    ELSE
        proclist [s↑.q].s := free;      (free one process free)
        s↑.q := proclist[s↑.q].l
    END
    END;

BEGIN
FOR cproc := 1 TO maxproc DO
    newprocess (?,?,?,proclist[cproc].p);
    proclist[cproc].s := free;
    proclist[cproc].l := 0
    END;

loop
    FOR cproc := 1 TO maxproc DO
        IF proclist[cproc].s = free THEN
            transfer (coord, proclist[cproc].p)
        END
    END
END
END;
```

16.7.4 Devices and interrupts

Actual control of devices is handled by allowing the programmer to specify the addresses of operands, thus mapping them on to the hardware control registers, for example,

    VAR disccr [177460B]: SET OF 0..15

This in itself is not a great breakthrough, but it is the method of handling interrupts that is of interest.

After writing to the device control register to enable interrupts, the procedure

    iotransfer (p1,p2,va)

is called, where p1 and p2 are variables of type PROCESS and va is the address of the interrupt vector for the device. The effect is similar to transfer (p1,p2) except that a return to p1 is prepared for later. When the interrupt actually occurs, a transfer (p2,p1) is executed automatically to bring control back to the device driver.

Obviously some masking of interrupts is needed; this is achieved by permitting each module to indicate the processor priority at which it should be run.

16.8 REFERENCES

P. Brinch Hansen (1976). 'The Solo Operating System in Processes, Monitors and Classes', *Software Practice and Experience*, Vol. 6, pp. 165-200.

C. A. R. Hoare (1974). 'Monitors; An Operating System Structuring Concept', *Communications of the ACM*, Vol. 17, pp. 549-557.

A. M. Lister and K. J. Maynard (1976). 'An Implementation of Monitors', *Software Practice and Experience*, Vol. 6, pp. 377-386.

N. Wirth (1977). 'Modula: A Language for Modular Programming', *Software Practice and Experience*, Vol. 7, pp. 3-36.

16.9 PROBLEMS

1. Compare and contrast the merits of monitors and semaphores for process synchronisations.

2. Describe the message switching system as used by the MUSS operating system. Explain how his system might be used to synchronise access to a shared segment where any number of processes are allowed to read the segment concurrently, but only one process at a time can alter it.

17 Job Control Systems

The aims and objectives of an operating system were considered in the opening chapters. The second part of this book has largely concentrated on the development of such systems, and we have seen some of the limitations and the need for compromise for specific requirements. However, for most computer users, there is no requirement to understand the workings of the operating system, which is treated simply as a sealed box. It is, however, necessary for the user to say how he wants his job to be run. To achieve this, the user gives instructions to the operating system in the form of job control statements. These commands form the user interface with the operating system.

Early job control systems developed in a rather ad hoc manner; features and facilities were added as the need for them was recognised. For this reason, many of the job control systems in use today exhibit features which are largely remnants of their recent evolution. An account of the evolution of job control languages is given by Barron (Barron and Jackson, 1972).

17.1 FUNCTIONS OF THE JOB CONTROL SYSTEM

Initial requirements for job control arose in connection with the first spooling systems. These were developed to make more efficient use of processor time, largely by taking certain decisions such as when to start a job, out of the hands of the operator. This eliminated the delays that were due to operator response times but meant that instructions previously given to the operators (scribbled on the back of a card deck or on special job submission forms) now had to be acted on by the operating system. The sort of instructions that might be relevant for a particular job, and which on early systems would be given directly to the operator, might be:

URGENT — RUN BEFORE LUNCHTIME — 2 MINS COMPUTING

LOAD FORTRAN COMPILER, FOLLOWED BY
  "PROGRAM DECK" (WHITE CARDS) IN READER 1
  "TEST DATA" (BLUE CARDS) IN READER 2
CLEAR HANDSWITCHES BEFORE STARTING
  IF IT HALTS DISPLAYING "777",
    SET HANDSWITCHES TO "101" AND CONTINUE.
STORE PRINTOUT IF ERROR OCCURS.

These instructions contain the rudiments of all the facilities that are included in present–day job control systems. The kind of information supplied can be classified into a number of different groups as follows:

(1) What the job does – for example, compile and run a Pascal program.

(2) The precise sequence of actions if a job consists of several separate steps – for example edit, compile, run.

(3) Special actions to be taken in the case of errors or other unusual conditions. Note that in manual systems, fault monitoring was very much the operator's responsibility.

(4) The resources required by the job. This information tends to fall into two categories.
   (a) Peripheral devices, etc., required. This information is used essentially for scheduling reasons so that a job is not started until all its resource requirements can be met. This is particularly important for magnetic tapes since a request for a particular tape might involve the operator walking to the basement to find it; so the system needs to request tapes well in advance of actually starting the job.
   (b) Restrictions on the resources needed by the job, particularly time, store, and output amounts. This is to prevent a looping job from consuming resources indefinitely; if it exceeds any of its stated limits it can be abandoned. This information can be used also for scheduling purposes; for example, by giving priority to short jobs.

(5) Special scheduling instructions – relative urgency of the job, any deadlines that must be met, etc.

(6) Parameters for this run. Programs can be written to do different

things depending on the setting of parameters. (In early systems, the main parameter was the handswitches.) Particularly important parameters are the specifications of what inputs and outputs are to be used so that the same program can be used without alterations on different kinds of input and output (for example, files, terminal input/output, cards, etc.).

It is worth noting that the above refers particularly to batch-oriented systems. In an interactive system, the emphasis is rather different. Certainly (1), (2) and (6) are still required, and are usually achieved by a sequence of 'commands' with associated parameters. Advance specification of error recovery actions (3) is not necessary, as the user can see if an error has occurred and take the appropriate action (by typing a command) himself. Resource requirements (4) are usually confined to the terminal and the user's files, which are made available automatically and need not be requested. Resource limits, to be useful, would have to refer to individual interactions. This is far too inconvenient for the user and so they are not usually specified. Scheduling instructions (5) are not usually necessary, the implication being that all jobs are urgent and all results wanted *now*. Some systems allow the user to specify the urgency of his work, and thus affect his response time.

17.2 TYPES OF JOB CONTROL LANGUAGE

Three different ways can be identified in which job control information can be supplied to the system:

1. As a 'job description' – a separate document containing all job control information (corresponding to the operator instructions in a manual system).

2. As a sequence of commands, written in a 'command language'.

3. As a program, incorporating commands as in (2) but with more sophisticated programming facilities (variables, control constructs, etc.) to 'steer' the job through error actions, etc.

The first of these three applies sensibly only to batch systems. It is now rather out of favour because most systems try to cater for both batch and interactive use through a single job control language. The second is by far the most common, corresponding directly to the needs of most interactive users. Sequencing of job steps is implicit, commands being executed in turn as they are typed. The third is necessary if a command-based system is to be used in a batch environment; error actions are then dealt with by using conditional statements (IF-THEN-ELSE or some other form). Sophisticated users can also make use of the ability to write loops and procedures in job control languages and even to use variables. The trend in command languages today is to use this technique which degenerates to the simple sequence of commands for most interactive users.

17.3 REQUIREMENTS OF JOB CONTROL LANGUAGES

Probably the most important requirement of any job control language is that it be convenient to use and easy to learn. Most users do not wish to waste time learning and using complex job control languages (though some masochists love to do just this!). Job control is a necessary evil not a superfacility, and this should be taken into account when designing job control languages. Nevertheless, a system must be sufficiently powerful to meet the needs of its most sophisticated users.

Convenience is achieved through a number of simple and rather obvious measures – above all, simplicity and uniformity. Commands should be brief (to minimise typing) but reasonably mnemonic (to minimise searching through manuals). They should preferably have few parameters, and wherever possible it should be permitted to miss out a parameter and obtain an installation-defined default. (Some systems even allow individual users to set their own defaults.)

There are two common ways in which parameters may be supplied. One is by position – the position in the list of parameters indicates which parameter is being specified. This is the normal method used in programming languages. The alternative is by keyword, giving a 'keyword' for each parameter. In the command:

GET, File name / UN = User name

there are two parameters, a file name (which is specified by position) and a user name (which is specified by keyword). The positional form has the advantage of minimising typing; the keyword form, however, is more convenient if there are many parameters, as (a) it is not necessary to remember the order of parameters, and (b) it is a simple matter to omit parameters and obtain defaults.

In an online system, informative prompting and error diagnostics can greatly simplify use of the system. A prompt serves to indicate that the machine is waiting for input – in general, there is no indication of what input it is waiting for. It would be much more useful if the prompt distinguished at least between (a) system commands, (b) edit commands and (c) input while inserting a new file or using the editor to insert text. In extreme cases the system would be able to issue a meaningful prompt for each parameter required (for example, TYPE FILE NAME).

Of course, the disadvantage of prompting is that experienced users become impatient while waiting for the system to print a lengthy prompt (particularly with slow, hard copy devices). Even on high speed terminals, prompting is annoying if the system takes some time to respond and print a prompt. The experienced user would then prefer to carry on typing, ahead of the system, rather than waiting for a prompt. For this reason many systems (a) prompt only if the user has not yet started typing, and (b) provide a terse mode of operation in which prompts are omitted and error diagnostics are cryptic.

Another feature common in online systems is an online user manual in the form of a HELP command. The user can request information about what commands are available and more detailed information about each individual command. Some systems will give a detailed explanation of exactly what is requested (similar to a prompt) if the user types a question-mark at any point.

17.4 ADDITIONAL FEATURES

'Additional' features of command languages are the features that allow job control to be expressed in a program-like form. The ability to declare and use variables (or in some cases, use without declaration) is provided in some systems. Also, the ability to direct control out of the normal sequence, using conditional and repetitive constructs. Some modern command languages resemble quite powerful programming languages, with built-in string manipulation facilities for handling parameters. Many of these are aimed not at the normal user but at people who provide further facilities for users. Often there is the ability to define new commands in terms of existing ones. In programming terms, this is the equivalent of a procedure. It is of great importance if ordinary users are to run complex jobs without being exposed to the complexities of the job control sequences involved. The complicated job control facilities thus provide the means whereby much simpler interfaces can be presented to the end user.

Another way in which new commands may be introduced is by writing programs in an ordinary programming language. In several systems, any program that a user compiles will automatically become a new command for that user. In Pascal, where each program has a heading specifying its parameters, commands with parameters could be produced. For example, if an editor was written with the program heading:

PROGRAM cjtedit (input, output, infile, outfile)

when compiled it could *automatically* become a new command cjtedit, with four (or, more usefully, two) parameters of type file. This could then be called from the command language, just as if it were a system command.

17.5 STANDARDISATION

With the widespread use of computers, it is now common for users to have access to several different computers. It would clearly be advantageous if some uniformity existed in the use of operating systems, as many people who have, for example, to cope with a diversity of text editors, will agree. Despite this, almost every operating system has its own command language, performing (largely) the same functions as other command languages but with a different vocabulary and syntax. Sometimes, two systems will even use the same command for different functions. Several standardisation efforts (Beech, 1979) have had little apparent success. Meanwhile every system designer perpetuates his own ideas in the absence of any clear guidance from the users. Usually the resulting system is a combination of things the designer has used and liked (or not used and missed!) in other systems.

Because of the lack of agreement on what command language should look like, it has been suggested that, as a start, the vocabulary (or a subset of it) be agreed on, so that all systems use the same words for common commands such as logging in, listing files, etc. This, together with a standard editor, would go a long way towards achieving the required uniformity, but it has not yet happened. Typical is the continued existence of the terms LOGIN or LOGON for connecting on to a system, and the corresponding LOGOUT or LOGOFF for logging out.

The problems of using different computers with different command languages, particularly in a network, have given rise to the development of several 'portable' command languages. These can be used with several existing operating systems, and work by translating commands in the portable system to the actual command language of the target machine. As yet, such systems have achieved only fairly localised use, but they do seem to offer the only way of achieving any form of standardisation using existing operating systems.

One further point is worth mentioning in this context. Several single-language interactive systems have achieved a high degree of standardisation by defining job control functions as part of the programming language definition. For example, the user of BASIC is normally presented with an identical user interface on any machine. This is true even when BASIC is provided as a subsystem of a general purpose system.

17.6 PROCEDURAL APPROACH TO JOB CONTROL

In early operating systems, the command language was an integral part of the system, and functions such as listing files, deleting files, etc., could be achieved only through the command language. This has two major disadvantages for the user:

(1) It is impossible to provide alternative command languages, or at least this can be done only by rewriting all of the programs and utilities that the commands invoke.

(2) It is very difficult for job control actions to be performed by programs. Sometimes it is desirable for a program to delete a file without the user having to type a command.

A more satisfactory approach is to separate the facilities of the system (that is, what it can do) from its command language (that is, how it is asked to do something). This can be done by defining the system's facilities as procedures, which can be called by any program. Such a system would have a comprehensive library of procedures to perform all the major job control functions; these would include compilers and editors as well as the other utility programs. The command interpreter is then just a program that calls on some library procedures. There is nothing particularly special about it and the system can if desired support several different command languages simultaneously, all accessing the same facilities. Indeed, if the user programming languages also allow calls to library procedures, it is possible to express job control requirements in ordinary programming languages.

The MUSS operating system takes this approach to its logical extreme. The command language consists simply of a sequence of procedure calls, supplying command name (procedure name) and parameters. All the interpreter has to do is read the command, find the relevant procedure in the library and enter it with the specified parameters. No knowledge of *what* the commands do is built into the interpreter, and no knowledge of command and parameter syntax is built into the command procedures. In this way, either can be modified independently of the other.

17.7 REFERENCES

D. W. Barron and I. R. Jackson, (1972). 'The evolution of job control language', *Software - Practice and Experience*, Vol. 2, pp. 143-164.

D. Beech (Ed.), (1979). 'Command Language Directions', *Proceedings of the 1979 IFIP Conference*, North-Holland.

17.8 PROBLEMS

1. Discuss the major functions and objectives of a job control command language, and the ways in which they may be achieved.

2. Discuss the main facilities required of a job control language, and show how they relate to features of the virtual machine.

3. How might a batch scheduling system, which aimed at improving machine efficiency by multiprogramming, use information given in the job control language?

Index

FUNDING HEALTH CARE:
2008 AND BEYOND

Report from the Leeds Castle summit